The Spacious Place

Kathy Erickson

ISBN-10: 1539460509
ISBN-13: 978-1539460503

DEDICATION

૭

This book is dedicated to my favorites: David, Sarah, Ben and Megan

CONTENTS

INTRODUCTION

When I was little, my grandmother used to pay me a dollar for each verse of the Bible I memorized. I jumped at the chance to get rich and went straight for the Psalms. Despite my consistent memorization, many of the Psalms seemed distant and inapplicable to my life. King David being chased by his enemies, his anguish for his sin, his deep passionate cries for help didn't resonate much with me as a unremarkable, middle class white kid in America. I identified more with the stories and characters of the Bible, the acts of bravery or cowardice, and the successes and failures of God's people. And, embarrassingly, I was more than a little preoccupied with impressing people and doing all I could to succeed by some worldly standard. I often found the Bible less interesting than the gossip column or my self-improvement efforts.

A few years back, I came to a crisis point in my life. I no longer could maintain a life that revolved around making everyone around me happy, only to come up short again and again. I was trying so hard to be acceptable to the world, and it wasn't impressed.

For the next several years, I struggled to find myself in the midst of pain, depression and anxiety which had accompanied this transformation. I needed to become my own person, with my own thoughts and opinions, even while knowing this would be unacceptable for some others. I had to accept that I would be spoken of negatively. Some people would not understand. Some would be hurt or angry. They might not like me anymore.

This Bible study is the result of those years of struggle. The Lord led me back to the Psalms and they became my refuge again and again. I so identified with David and the Psalmists now. God took me out of this place where I was open, exposed and vulnerable to attack and placed me in a protective place of safety. It was a hiding place where, for a time, I was a bit isolated in order to be healed by Him. But God did not leave me there. Time and again God brought me back to Psalm 31, especially verse 8:

> You have not handed me over to the enemy
> but have set my feet in a spacious place.

I am so thankful for the spacious place in which God has placed me. It is a place of freedom, peace, acceptance, protection, truth and transformation. It is here I can feel my shoulders relax and I can breathe. It is here I know I am just loved for who I am, not for what I do.

In this study we are going to examine what the spacious place is like, and what it is not like. We will look at our own lives to see if we are taking advantage of this amazing blessing, and we will learn how to live in the spacious place. I hope to share with you the joy and peace God has given me through my struggles. By claiming the promise of the spacious place, you have access to a tool in dealing with the struggles that will come to you in your personal journey in life.

Join me as we enter this beautiful place, open to us all, available for the taking. God desires for you to rest here, and accept Him as your healer, comforter, and as the One who loves your soul like no one else can. Let's join Him there.

A few notes about the format of this study:

- Each week contains five days of study.
- At the end of each week, I encourage you to get together with a group to share what God is teaching you.
- In each day's lesson, certain questions are designated with bold print. These questions are ones I would suggest your group makes sure to cover during your discussions. If you are struggling to finish the lessons, these bolded questions can help you know what will be discussed.
- Each week focuses on a different Bible character or characters. We will study them for a week and see how their lives illustrate an aspect of the spacious place.
- The topics for the week are formatted as a contrasting pair. My hope is by looking at what the spacious place should not be and what it could be, we will grow to understand the possibilities of what it could be like to live in the spacious place. (I promise I will explain the concept more as we dig into the study!)
- If you are doing the study alone, consider asking a friend if you can share with him or her what you are learning. Forming your own ideas and thoughts into sentences can help you clarify and remember what you are learning.
- I have used the NIV(1984) translation throughout the study. Any translation you want to use will work for almost every question. I have capitalized the pronouns referring to God everywhere except the scripture passages, where I left the format the same as the translation.

WEEK 1: THE SPACIOUS PLACE

One of my favorite books as a child was *The Secret Garden*, by Frances Hodgson Burnett. Do you remember the story? A little girl, Mary, was born in India to British parents and was orphaned. She went back to England to live with a wealthy relative and his crippled son. Both the father and son were wounded, hurting and broken-hearted people. Mary herself was difficult, self-absorbed, and wrapped up in her own sorrow.

The healing in the story came as Mary discovered and tended to a secret garden. As the plants bloomed into health and beauty, so did the characters in the book. As a girl, I was so intrigued by the thought of a secret place which could be all mine, a place where I was free to sing and dance and play; a place of beauty, love and safety. I loved picturing the garden, fresh and cool, blooming with fragrant flowers. I imagined the colors as bright and vibrant.

Did you have such dreams as a child? Did you have a secret place in your mind where you escaped when times were difficult or discouraging? I consider it a gift to have had a vivid imagination as a child. Sometimes as an adult, the realities of life, and the demands of maturity push those safe places out.

This week we'll start to get a handle on what living in the spacious place can look like, and revisit the imaginations of our yesterdays. Be ready to dream a little. It isn't childish, it's child-like and God can use it to teach you if you'll let Him.

MEMORY VERSE:

> *I will be glad and rejoice in your love, for you saw my affliction and knew the*
>
> *anguish of my soul. You have not handed me over to the enemy but have set my*
>
> *feet in a spacious place.*
>
> ☙ *Psalm 31:7-8*

3

❧ # Day 1 ❧

Commitment to the Promise

This is my prayer for you as you embark on this study. **As you read it, list in the margins the words Paul uses to describe our great God.**

Ephesians 1:17-23

I keep asking that the God of our Lord Jesus Christ, the glorious Father, may give you the Spirit of wisdom and revelation, so that you may know him better. I pray also that the eyes of your heart may be enlightened in order that you may know the hope to which he has called you, the riches of his glorious inheritance in the saints, and his incomparably great power for us who believe. That power is like the working of his mighty strength, which he exerted in Christ when he raised him from the dead and seated him at his right hand in the heavenly realms, far above all rule and authority, power and dominion, and every title that can be given, not only in the present age but also in the one to come. And God placed all things under his feet and appointed him to be head over everything for the church, which is his body, the fullness of him who fills everything in every way.

My desires for those who take on this study are similar to those desires Paul had for the Ephesians in the first part of this passage.

1. I desire for you to have the Spirit of wisdom and revelation.

2. I desire for you to know Him better.

3. I desire for this Bible study to enlighten you in some way through the work of the Holy Spirit.

4. I desire for you to know hope.

5. I desire for you to know you are called by God.

6. I desire for you to know the riches of your inheritance.

7. I desire for you to see His great power.

8. I desire for you to trust in His great power.

Which of these do you need most? Circle the number of the one that tugs at your heart, that is a thirst in your soul. We will revisit this prayer at the end of the study.

Read Ephesians 1:17-23 again. This time mark in orange references to God's power. This is a simple but important question. Does Paul believe God is powerful enough to answer his prayer for the Ephesians?

How about you? If you do believe it, are you living life as if you believe it? I'd like for you to do something you might not do often, pray for yourself! Use the paraphrase below to pray Ephesians 1:17-19a for yourself.

I keep asking that the God of our Lord Jesus Christ, the glorious

Father, may give me the Spirit of wisdom and revelation, so that I

may know Him better. I pray also that the eyes of my heart may be

enlightened in order that I may know the hope to which He has

5

called me, the riches of his glorious inheritance in the saints, and His incomparably great power for us who believe.

Response and/or prayer:

Day 2

The Tightrope

When I went off to college right after high school, I noticed right away not everyone did things the way I did. My roommates went to bed at different times than I did, they played their music at different volumes than I did, and they approached life, studies, celebrations and struggles differently than I did. And I was surprised! I was a little shocked not everyone did life the way I had been taught. I was tempted (and often succumbed to the temptation) to be judgmental. I thought if only they had thought about it, they would see I was right. It made for a lonely time.

When I accepted their habits or adopted them myself, I felt guilty I was turning against my family in some way. When I was around my friends, I was careful to either adopt their ways, or defend my own. When I was with my family, I reverted to their ways, not wanting to offend or experience disapproval. I began to walk on a tightrope. I became talented at guessing what other people were thinking. I could anticipate their responses and adjust my behavior to gain their approval. What I didn't do is figure out my own opinions and preferences. I was too busy walking the tightrope, desperate not to take a misstep.

The tightrope had nothing to do with right or wrong. It was not from God! It had everything to do with traditions, habits, and preferences. When I first started dating my husband, Dave, he made an innocent comment. He remarked how nice and kind a current political figure and his wife were. Immediately I broke up with him! It wasn't because I disapproved of that politician, it was because I knew my family's view of him. Immediately I could see clearly I would not be able to keep walking on the tightrope around my family when this boy would obviously offend them. I'm so thankful Dave talked me out of it, but my first response was to simply run away from conflict.

When Jesus interacted with the Pharisees, they too were busy walking on tightropes. The Pharisees were a group of religious people, and also a political party with influence in the Sanhedrin. The Sanhedrin was the supreme court and legislative body of the Jews. The Pharisees were careful followers of the laws and traditions, so careful, in fact, they had added rules of their own. All in all, they were carefully following 613 laws They were especially concerned with laws regarding tithing and ritual purity.

Read Exodus 30:19-21.

For whom did the Lord require hand washing and for what activities were they to be clean?

Numbers 18:8-13 extends the requirement for ceremonial cleansing beyond just for the priestly duties. Now they are also supposed to be ceremonially clean when they do what?

Were they required to be ceremonially clean before eating anything or was it when eating specific kinds of foods?

The Old Testament law did **not** require hand washing before meals. This was a tradition, and by the time of Jesus, so many more requirements had been added, the laws had become a burden to follow.

Let's look at an interaction between Jesus and the Pharisees. Read Luke 11:37-54. If you write in your Bible, circle all the "woe to you"s.

List all the actions of the Pharisees Jesus criticized.

What a list! I'll bet they were more than a little surprised at His response to them.

What were the concerns (priorities) of the Pharisees in this passage? List as many as you see or can infer from both the actions of the Pharisees and the words Jesus uses to describe them.

Now look at your list and circle any that were also a top concern for Jesus. These two parties clearly did not have the same concerns. Maybe this was why Jesus couldn't convince them and they walked away unchanged.

If you had been a Pharisee, raised in those traditions and following those laws, what do you think would be your biggest stumbling block to the message Jesus gave them? Why?

Look at the last verses in the passage. Not only were the Pharisees walking on a tightrope and working hard to stay on it, they also assumed Jesus was walking on a tightrope too. They thought if they could knock Him off, it would prove their ways were right. The spacious place is nowhere near a tightrope! Walking on a tightrope is NOT God's idea of what your life will look like when you follow Him. Learning about the spacious place can free you from the tightrope.

Are you ready to hear God's word for you? What will your response to Him be? Will you cling tighter to your ways and opinions? Or will you be open to hearing from Him what He might have to say to you in this Bible study? Write a prayer of commitment to Him. Consider the possibility He may have some things to say to you and they could be difficult to hear. Ask Him for courage to stop walking the tightrope and follow Him wherever He may lead.

Response and/or prayer:

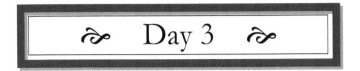

Imagining an Alternative

I have lived in many places around the United States, so I don't really have a "hometown." The one state where I've spent the most time in is Wisconsin. My husband and I lived there for three years at the beginning of our marriage and returned several years later for an eight year stint. I love Wisconsin, the beauty, the people, the lakes, and the Green Bay Packers. But I have to admit the winters were difficult for me. I don't like any winter sports, I don't enjoy being cold and more than anything, I miss seeing color in those gray and dreary months. We decided as much as we could swing it, we needed to plan a trip to someplace warm every February.

I remember one trip in particular when I stepped out of the airport doors in Florida. It took my breath away when I felt the warm air on my skin. My shoulders suddenly relaxed. I hadn't even known my shoulders were tense. My whole body had been tensed against the winter cold for months. I took a deep breath, closed my eyes and raised my face to the sun.

What a beautiful moment it was. The Wisconsin winter had taken a toll on me and I hadn't even known. I was tense, braced against the elements and trudging through. When you get used to the sub-zero temperatures, snow-covered landscape and icy roads, it's easy to forget a life could exist that is relaxed, colorful and warm.

I've spent too much of my life living in a winter state of mind, looking only at the bleak landscape of life, at the evil and at disappointments. I have braced myself against the struggles, and I have found myself living in a state of nervousness, anxiety, depression and hurt. If no one else would feel sorry for me, I'd have to do it myself!

And then God showed me the gift of the spacious place. (Psalm 31:8). For me accepting God's gift of the spacious place is like walking out those doors of the Florida airport, breathing in a huge gulp of fresh, warm air, feeling my shoulders relax and turning my face to the sun. It is a place of safety and love.

Your experience of a restful place may be different from mine. For those who live in a desert, maybe cool air or a wonderful rain shower is the picture of relief for you. For those who live in humid and hot climates, maybe it is the cool, dry air of the mountains. Maybe you love snowy, cold winters!

For the Israelites, their difficult climate was very different from mine. Read Exodus 15:22-23. What were the Israelites longing for?

Read Exodus 16:2-3. What were the Israelites longing for here?

Read Exodus 32:1. The Israelites turned to a golden calf in this verse. They missed Moses and didn't know what had happened to him. What did Moses provide that the people yearned for when he was gone?

In the following passages, list what God provided for them in each passage:

Exodus 15:27	
Exodus 16:4	
Exodus 40:36-38	

God met the needs of the Israelites in specific ways. He heard their cry for help and provided them in their moment of need. Look at the list below and circle at least three of these characteristics that represent a harsh world or climate for you in particular, or add ones of your own.

Bitter	Icy
Frigid	Humid
White	Hot

You have not handed me over to the enemy but have set my feet in a spacious place.

Cold	Barren
Rainy	Oppressive
Snowy	Bleak
Desolate	Forsaken
Lonely	Wild
Crowded	Crammed
Polluted	Swarming
Unrelenting	Dark
Noisy	Cacophonous
Silent	Blinding

Now imagine the alternative. **Think of words that represent the opposite of the words you circled.**

Copy Isaiah 58:11 here:

Now personalized this verse for yourself. Here's mine as an example:

The Lord will guide you always, Kathy. He will satisfy your needs in the darkest part of winter, and he will strengthen your frame. You will be like Florida in February, where the beauty of the Lord is obvious, your pace is restful and you are removed from your normal worries.

Write yours below:

13

Take a moment to imagine what picture of relief God is giving you. Sit in it for a moment.

What do you see?

What do you feel on your skin?

What do you hear?

What foods would you be able to eat here?

What lovely smells are in this place?

Can you feel the tension leave your body? God wants to lead you into a spacious place to live, not just visit on vacation. If your computer is full of digital pictures like mine is, or if you have boxes of pictures, look for a picture to represent your spacious place to you. Find a place to post it or make it the wallpaper on your computer while you complete this study.

You have not handed me over to the enemy but have set my feet in a spacious place.

Response and/or prayer:

ふ Day 4 ふ

Psalm 31

During some of the most difficult days the Lord has repeatedly brought me back to Psalm 31. It has given me great comfort and rest. Today I'd like to lead you through the psalm and invite you to experience it for yourself. The psalm is included below so you can mark it up and interact with it. Feel free to mark in the margins of your own Bible if you prefer.

First, read the psalm slowly, aloud if you can, underlining or circling anything that catches your eye or your heart. At the end of the psalm, I'll have some more specific instructions for you.

Psalm 31
For the director of music. A psalm of David.

1 In you, O LORD, I have taken my refuge;

let me never be put to shame;

deliver me in your righteousness.

2 Turn your ear to me,

come quickly to my rescue;

be my rock of refuge,

a strong fortress to save me.

3 Since you are my rock and my fortress,

for the sake of your name lead and guide me.

4 Free me from the trap that is set for me,

for you are my refuge.

5 Into your hands I commit my spirit;

redeem me, O LORD, the God of truth.

6 I hate those who cling to worthless idols;

I trust in the LORD.

7 I will be glad and rejoice in your love,

for you saw my affliction

and knew the anguish of my soul.

8 You have not handed me over to the enemy

but have set my feet in a spacious place.

9 Be merciful to me, O LORD, for I am in distress;

my eyes grow weak with sorrow,

my soul and my body with grief.

10 My life is consumed by anguish

and my years by groaning;

my strength fails because of my affliction,

and my bones grow weak.

11 Because of all my enemies,

I am the utter contempt of my neighbors;

I am a dread to my friends –

those who see me on the street flee from me.

12 I am forgotten by them as though I were dead;

I have become like broken pottery.

13 For I hear the slander of many;

there is terror on every side;

they conspire against me

and plot to take my life.

14 But I trust in you, O LORD;

I say, "You are my God."

15 My times are in your hands;

deliver me from my enemies

and from those who pursue me.

16 Let your face shine on your servant;

save me in your unfailing love.

17 Let me not be put to shame, O LORD,

for I have cried out to you;

but let the wicked be put to shame

and lie silent in the grave.

18 Let their lying lips be silenced,

for with pride and contempt

they speak arrogantly against the righteous.

19 How great is your goodness,

which you have stored up for those who fear you,

which you bestow in the sight of men

on those who take refuge in you.

20 In the shelter of your presence you hide them

from the intrigues of men;

in your dwelling you keep them safe

from accusing tongues.

21 Praise be to the LORD,

for he showed his wonderful love to me

when I was in a besieged city.

22 In my alarm I said,

"I am cut off from your sight!"

yet you heard my cry for mercy

when I called to you for help.

23 Love the LORD, all his saints!

The LORD preserves the faithful,

but the proud he pays back in full.

24 Be strong and take heart,

all you who hope in the LORD.

With **red**, mark all the references to the evil that are happening to David in this passage.

With **blue**, mark all references to David's enemies and their actions. (We will look back at this another day.)

With **green**, mark all the attributes of God David mentions.

Make a list of what you learn about God from this psalm.

The last verse is David's advice to the reader. What is he saying to you?

Finally, with yellow, underline the one verse (or verses) that speaks most clearly to your heart. Pick one attribute of God to meditate on and think about today. Write it on a note card and carry it with you throughout this week.

Response and/or prayer:

Identifying Enemies

Psalm 31 was written by David. In his lifetime, David was continually confronted with clear enemies. From the Philistines and their giant Goliath, to Saul, to the Amalekites, to Saul again, David's enemies seem clear. As king of Judah and then Israel, David's enemies were political. He was often fleeing for his life in a literal way. Satan used these enemies to attack David and God's kingdom. This is why for many years I didn't feel I had much to gain from the Psalms. No one was chasing me through the desert, throwing spears at me or trying to defeat my kingdom.

Our ultimate enemy is of course Satan and his demons. First Peter 5:8b says, "Your enemy the devil prowls around like a roaring lion looking for someone to devour." Satan is oh so subtle at times. He uses all kinds of distractions and opposition to take our eyes off the Father. Let's broaden our understanding of the kinds of enemies Satan puts in our path. What if we categorized our enemies in this way?

1. **Physical enemies**: those people or things that are trying to hurt you physically

2. **Social enemies**: those who hurt with gossip, untruth, slander and hurtful words or attitudes (can be intentional or unintentional)

3. **Emotional enemies**: internal patterns of thinking or feeling that are unhealthy and harmful

4. **Spiritual enemies**: struggles and temptations that draw us away from God or breed doubt in our minds

Look back over your marked up copy of Psalm 31 from yesterday. You marked all the references to David's enemies in blue. Look at each reference and mark it with a 1, 2, 3, or 4 according to what kind of enemy you think David could have been facing. Some of them are vague and can have more than one possibility. All of them are being used by our ultimate enemy.

What kind of enemy do you think David is primarily facing in this psalm? Is it surprising?

Notice of the four types of enemies, not all of them are people. And even the ones that are people, may not be caused by people who are purposefully trying to hurt you. This is not to excuse those who abuse or hurt. I only want us to think beyond the narrow idea that our enemies are people who are out to get us.

For me, at times, my own emotions and gut reactions have been enemies I've needed to battle. If you are telling yourself untrue lies about yourself, your words are your enemy. If you feel guilt for things that are not your responsibility, your guilty feeling is your enemy. If you have sin in your life that plagues you, then that temptation, that sin is your enemy. If you have people in your life who hurt your feelings, degrade or diminish you and your worth, then they are your enemy. It doesn't mean they can't also be people you love.

Think through each of the categories of enemies we have talked about. Jot down the initials of people in your life now and in your past who may fall into these categories. Jot down any other enemies you have battled or are battling now.

1. Physical enemies:

2. Social enemies

You have not handed me over to the enemy but have set my feet in a spacious place.

3. Emotional enemies

4. Spiritual enemies

Now copy down Psalm 31:7-8 in light of the enemies you have faced and are facing right now.

Do you remember the spacious place you imagined for yourself in day 2? Look back if you need to refresh your memory. Then take a moment to picture yourself right now. Visualize yourself battling an enemy you face. Now see God gathering you up, removing you from that enemy, and setting you down in your spacious place. Close your eyes and feel the relief. **Take some time to thank Him for not leaving you to battle your enemies alone.**

Response and/or prayer:

WEEK 2: FREEDOM NOT SLAVERY

I have come to realize I am a perfectionist. Now, please know my house is not perfect, my children are not robots, and I am not always meticulously groomed. The way my perfectionism manifests itself is in how I *feel* about my imperfect home, my childish children, my appearance and actions.

One day I needed to renew two prescriptions at the local pharmacy. I requested the prescriptions but before I could pick them up I got an automated call from the pharmacy saying there was a delay with one of the drugs. No problem, I wasn't in desperate need of the medications, so I didn't pick up either of them. A couple of days passed when I got another automated call from the pharmacy. The voice informed me if I didn't pick up my prescriptions within twenty-four hours they would be re-shelved.

Now I would imagine most people would take this for what it was, a reminder to get to the pharmacy and pick up the medications. But I got angry. I felt reprimanded by the automated voice and I did not like it at all. My thoughts were obsessed with how the pharmacy was at fault. I never received a call saying the problem was resolved and the prescriptions were ready. I really stewed over this. I contemplated complaining to the pharmacy staff and alerting them of their "mistake." I certainly didn't want the blame on me.

I feel awful when I make mistakes, but when blamed for something that is not my fault, I get angry. The ultimate pain for me is having others think poorly of me. It steamed me that some pharmacy worker might think I was negligent, or irresponsible. Really, the amount of time and energy I expended thinking all these thoughts was outrageous. Though it has been several years, I remember how it felt clearly.

This is one of the ways I have lived like an enslaved person, not a free person. I was walking on a tightrope of these narrowly defined rules about being "good." The crazy thing is none of these rules were biblical. They were rules I bought into somehow. I believed I should not be a person who forgets things, or who makes mistakes, or who says the wrong thing. And I was miserable. All the while God was offering me an alternative and I was turning away from His offer.

The spacious place into which God places us is a place of freedom and not a place of slavery. Our main focus this week will be on Galatians 4:21-31 which refers back to the stories of Sarah and Hagar in the Old Testament. When God calls us to live a life of freedom and promise but we choose to live a life of slavery, well, what a heartbreaking choice that is. It is like what the Galatians were doing when Paul confronts them in his letter.

Having seen the freedom and blessing of grace, they were choosing instead to live under the law. I'm praying you will see some new things about yourself and your relationship with God this week!

MEMORY VERSE:

> *Therefore, there is now no condemnation for those who are in Christ Jesus,*
>
> *because through Christ Jesus the law of the Spirit of life set me free from the law*
>
> *of sin and death.*
>
>   *Romans 8:1-2*

Sarah

The passage we will study this week in Galatians 4 is a particularly hard passage to understand. So before we go there, we need to gather some knowledge Paul assumed his audience would already have. We are going to start with Sarah's story.

The first mention of Sarah (her original name is Sarai) is found in Genesis 11:27-32. Read this passage and list anything you learn about Sarah.

Continue to read the story in Genesis 12. What was Abraham promised by God? (vs. 2-3)

Where did they move next and who went with them?

You have not handed me over to the enemy but have set my feet in a spacious place.

Why did the family continue on to Egypt? (vs. 10)

Imagine you are Sarah. **How do you think she felt about the events in verses 10-17?**

Let's skip ahead a couple of chapters to Genesis 16. By now God has again told Abraham about the promise of a great nation, coming from a natural born son. And yet the years were passing and Sarah remained barren.

Read Genesis 16:1-6. Whom did Sarah blame for her fertility?

This is an important clue to Sarah's state of mind and her motives behind her next actions. **What did Sarah assume would have to happen for Gods' promise to be fulfilled?**

This practice of giving a maidservant to the husband in order to produce heirs was a common practice at this time. The children born of the union were considered to be the children of the wife, not of the maidservant. Soon the situation soured between Hagar and Sarah.

What does the text say about how Hagar behaved toward Sarah? (vs. 4b)

What does the text say about how Sarah behaved toward Hagar? (vs. 6b)

Which character in the story do you think was most at fault? Why?

I know there was a lot of reading today, so good job getting through it all! I hope you have a better sense of Sarah, her life, her experiences and her motives. It is important to remember these were real people with real feelings and real experiences. Tomorrow we will talk more about Hagar and look at her side of the story.

Response and/or prayer:

You have not handed me over to the enemy but have set my feet in a spacious place.

∾ **Day 2** ∾

Hagar

Yesterday we looked at the life of Sarah and ended when her relationship with Hagar, the maidservant, was becoming difficult or even unbearable. Let's pick up the story as Hagar flees from her mistress, Sarah.

Based on the first six verses of Genesis 16 we read yesterday, describe the situation in which Hagar finds herself.

Now read Genesis 16:6-16. (The location of the road to Shur is debated, but it is likely a road back to Egypt, Hagar's home.) The angel of the Lord found Hagar and spoke to her. Complete the following sentences:

The angel of the Lord knew...

The angel asked Hagar...

The angel told Hagar to go...

You have not handed me over to the enemy but have set my feet in a spacious place.

The angel told Hagar to act...

Just as Abraham had been given a promise from God regarding his family, so Hagar also gets a promise from the angel. What are the elements of her promise?

Remember the custom for this type of surrogacy was the child would be handed over to the wife and would be considered hers. The angel made it clear this was not to be. (see vs. 11) So Sarah's plan has failed to give her a child.

Read vs. 13-14 again. **What do these verses and this whole passage reveal about our great God?**

What was Hagar's reaction to the visit with the angel?

Let's really try to put ourselves in the places of Sarah and Hagar. Write an S next to any emotions you would imagine Sarah might have felt in any of the circumstances we read about. Write an H next to any emotions Hagar might have had.

- anger
- jealousy
- joy
- sadness
- disappointment
- discouragement
- despair
- fear
- trust
- disgust
- surprise
- anticipation
- love
- awe
- remorse
- pride
- contempt
- loss
- anxiety
- compassion
- envy
- doubt
- frustration

Which emotion or event strikes you most? Have you had a situation in which you've felt like Sarah or Hagar? Did it lead you towards God or away from Him?

The stories for these two women wrap up in Genesis 21. Read verses 1-21. God clearly cares for Abraham and Sarah and blesses them with the birth of Isaac. But the surprise in the story is He also cares deeply for Hagar, the slave, and provides for her needs and for her son. God was with him as he grew up.

Now that we have established the basic facts, we can now look at Galatians and see how Paul read and interpreted the story. Thanks for sticking with me through this background study. Whether you identify most with Sarah or with Hagar, I believe God can speak to you and your situation through this.

With which character in these passages do you identify most?

Do you desire God to do for you what he did for Sarah or Hagar? In what way(s)?

Response and/or prayer:

You have not handed me over to the enemy but have set my feet in a spacious place.

Paul's Illustration

The book of Galatians is all about grace. One of the central issues for the early church was how to live as a Christian if you were a Jew first, and how to live as a Christian if you were a Gentile first. The church in Galatia was being influenced by a group of people who were insisting Christ followers must also continue to follow the Jewish laws and customs. The issue at hand is circumcision, which may seem like an irrelevant question for modern people. But the more basic questions is still essential for us each to answer today:

On what can I rely to make me right before God?

Like during Paul's time, today people rely on many things other than the work of Jesus on the cross. More than any other, I see people relying on themselves and on their ability to be "good" to save them.

So Paul is arguing throughout Galatians there is a better way to live than to be enslaved to laws and rituals. He wants them to choose freedom instead of slavery. In Galatians 4:21-31, he uses the stories we've just spent the last two days dissecting to illustrate his point.

Read Galatians 4:21-31.

Let me take a minute to say I do not believe Paul is denying or downplaying the historicity of the events in Sarah's and Hagar's lives. I believe he is using their lives as an illustration. He sees the historical facts in some way embody the theological point he is making. It is quite a brilliant illustration really.

Let's look at the contrast:

	Sarah	**Hagar**
Status	Free	Slave
Promise	New covenant	Sinai covenant

Legacy	Jerusalem from above (eternal)	Present Jerusalem (temporary)
Sons	Isaac	Ishmael
Birth	Through a promise, supernatural	Ordinary (flesh), natural
Actions of the Sons	Persecuted	Persecutor
Result	Heir	Outcast

Now if you are like me, you may be objecting to Paul's contrasts. Poor Hagar! He seems portraying Hagar as the "bad guy" with a promise that was temporary, and a son destined to have a conflict ridden life. It seems to me the real life complexities of the story are a bit more grey and a little less black and white. But what I think Paul is doing here is drawing a contrast in order to point out the absurdity of what the Galatians were doing.

Considering whom Paul is addressing in Galatians (see vs. 21), why do you suppose he chose this particular illustration?

What happened on Mount Sinai? (see Exodus 19:2-3)

How does this event relate to Hagar in Galatians 5:24-25?

You have not handed me over to the enemy but have set my feet in a spacious place.

Whom does Paul consider to be slaves in his time in history? (see Galatians 4:8)

Paul accuses one group of persecuting another. Who is persecuting whom? (Galatians 4:28-29)

Paul seems a little angry here! Read Acts 13:49-52. Does the treatment Paul and Barnabas received from the Jews shed some light on Paul's anger? How?

In verse 31, the word "therefore" indicates Paul is drawing his conclusion. What is it?

What do you think that means for you?

Write the next verse (Galatians 5:1) here:

Those of us who are relying on Christ for our salvation have been FREED from a yoke of slavery. And yet, like those in the church in Galatia, many of us are still living like we are slaves and not like we are free people. God's promise of the spacious place offers us a status of freedom. So when we live like we are still enslaved, we are rejecting His promise.

What is holding you captive? How can you break free?

Tomorrow we'll talk more about how this can manifest itself in our modern lives. Great job today! This is a difficult passage.

Response and/or prayer:

You have not handed me over to the enemy but have set my feet in a spacious place.

இ Day 4 இ

Slavery

Each of us, before we came to Christ, was like a slave. We were slaves to our sin, or slaves to our attempts to be good enough. Isn't that interesting? We can be slaves to both ends of the spectrum.

<u>Complete depravity</u>   <u>Complete religiosity</u>
Slave to sin   Slave to self

Anywhere on this continuum we can find ourselves enslaved. Consider a person with an addiction issue. That person is enslaved in a real and observable way. The use of a substance, food, sex or shopping feels like a compulsion they can't control. But also consider a person who appears holy on the outside. Any time we stop relying on God we are enslaved.

Read Romans 6. This chapter is all about freedom we should have as Christ followers and how we continue in slavery despite that. Fill in the blanks below from verse 16.

Don't you know that when you offer yourselves to someone to

obey him as slaves, you are _____ to the one whom

you_____ - whether you are slaves to _____,

which leads to _____, or to _____,

which leads to _____.

Identify a verse in Romans 6 that helps you understand Paul's message regarding slavery and freedom. What does it mean in your own words?

You have not handed me over to the enemy but have set my feet in a spacious place.

Look at this list of types of slavery. Put a mark by any that strike you as ones you are struggling with or have struggled with in the past.

Types of slavery:

- slavery to sin
- slavery to a behavior
- slavery to expectations and opinions of others
- slavery to your own expectations
- slavery to religion, rules, traditions
- slavery to fear or anxiety
- slavery to shame
- slavery to the idols of the world (fame, money, power, pleasure)
- slavery to sorrow and grief
- slavery to bitterness, anger, or hurt

Let's try to identify some of the things that may be enslaving you, even if they aren't obvious to you.

What keeps your mind earth bound? What blocks you from having a perspective that focuses on God's ultimate plan rather than on your immediate situation?

What makes you feel most worried or discouraged?

I follow many rules that are not required by God, but are ones I require of myself because of my own need for approval. I must always be on time. I must never forget appointments. My home must be clean to have company. I must have a clean car.

Name a rule you follow that is NOT something God requires of you.

What do you do to free yourself from powerful emotions? What do you do to pull yourself out of despair or frustration or discouragement?

If I were to look at your bank account, checkbook, or credit card receipts, what would I conclude about what is most important to you?

If I were to analyze your calendar, what would I conclude about what is most important to you?

Now look back at your answers and prayerfully try to identify an area that may be keeping you from experiencing God's freedom of the spacious place.

Remember Psalm 31:8:

> You have not handed me over to the enemy
> but have set my feet in a spacious place.

Whatever enslaves you is your enemy and God can save you from that enemy and set you in a place of freedom if you let Him. Spend some time in prayer today talking with God about what you learned. Don't be discouraged if you feel thoroughly enslaved. When God takes on a tough case, His glory shines even brighter. Remember He is bigger and stronger than anything you or I can deal with alone.

Response and/or prayer:

Freedom

Look back and remind yourself of the spacious place you imagined for yourself in the first week. Write down three key words that describe your version of the spacious place:

1.

2.

3.

Now imagine a huge stone wall being built in the middle of the space. You are on one side of the wall and God is on the other. The builders are putting it up so quickly and skillfully that you have no hope of going over, under or around it. You no longer can see God, just the wall. That's what spiritual slavery looks like. It blocks us from seeing God, separates us from Him and occupies our focus. We can get so used to the existence of the wall in our lives we forget about God. We forget there is something much better on the other side. AND, we forget the wall is optional; it doesn't have to be there.

Read Isaiah 61:1-3 below. This is a prophecy about the ministry Jesus came to accomplish on earth.

Hear Jesus speaking to you about what He can do, and underline or highlight the concepts God wants for you to hear today.

The Spirit of the Sovereign Lord is on me, because the Lord has

anointed me to preach good news to the poor. He has sent me to

bind up the brokenhearted, to proclaim freedom for the captives

and release from darkness for the prisoners, to proclaim the year of

the Lord's favor and the day of vengeance of our God, to comfort all who mourn, and provide for those who grieve in Zion – to

bestow on them a crown of beauty instead of ashes, the oil of

gladness instead of mourning, and a garment of praise instead of a

spirit of despair. They will be called oaks of righteousness, a planting

of the Lord for the display of his splendor.

One of the (many) struggles I deal with in my life is the desire to have others like me. I want so badly for everyone in my life to think highly of me, to see I am a good person, to agree with the decisions I make and to understand my heart.

Well, in the REAL WORLD...that doesn't always happen. In real life people misunderstand me or disagree with me. They honk at me on the road, they question my motives and sometimes refuse to be understanding. Sometimes they even find me annoying. Imagine that!

I remember a specific day when my first child was just a baby. I was so upset by something someone had said to me I put the baby in the car and went driving. I was crying and having intense arguments with people in my head. It took me hours to calm down. I remember feeling I had to get away from what I was feeling; it was too intense. That's why I drove. I was enslaved to the feelings that were pouring over me and I struggled to feel God was right there ready to help me.

Our posture during crisis is so key. Is our posture turned with our back to God? Do we run away from the problem, the feelings, the issue and from God? Or is our posture turned toward God? Do we turn to Him and allow Him to carry us through?

Can you think of a time you adopted either posture (towards God or running away)? What happened?

Now look at the next verse in Isaiah 61, verse 4:

They will rebuild the ancient ruins and restore the places long devastated; they will renew the ruined cities that have been

devastated for generations.

It seems to me there is a process to gaining freedom in your life. Let's continue to think about the metaphor of the spacious place with a wall in the middle separating us from God. That wall probably isn't going to disappear in an instant. Our God is certainly strong enough to make it disappear, but I think sometimes the journey through it is where He wants us to go. Imagine God demolishing the wall. What would be left? Ruins.

So even after we ask Him to help us conquer our enslavements and remove them from our lives, we may be left with a mess. That mess may represent broken relationships, hurt feelings, feelings of loss and loneliness. It may represent grief as you give up something that has been part of your life for years. Look again at the verse in Isaiah 61:4.

List the verbs or actions in this verse: (Hint: in the NIV they all start with R)

1.

2.

3.

How do these verbs make you feel? What emotions do they evoke?

Dare to dream about what your life might look like if your enslavements were destroyed and your spacious place was renewed. **How might your life be different?**

As we wrap up this week, find some time to pray, even if you don't feel comfortable doing it. If writing down your prayers helps you, do that. If kneeling helps you, do that. If walking in nature helps you speak to God, do that.

- Ask God to help you see the walls that are keeping you prisoner.
- Ask Him to give you the courage to imagine His vision for your life.
- Ask Him to tear down those walls and walk with you through the possibly painful process.
- Then ask Him to rebuild, restore and renew you.
- Ask Him to help you live in the freedom of the spacious place.

Response and/or prayer:

WEEK 3: PEACE NOT ANXIETY

We usually take one big family trip each year for vacation. These trips are great, but one year we decided to depart from the norm and try something different. We took each of our kids on a one-on-one trip alone with just Mom or Dad. My daughter and I flew across the country to Hollywood. We visited a theme park, took a tour of a movie studio and spent a day on the beach. All of our kids talk about those trips more than any others we have done.

The memories are great...except one. I tend to be an anxious flier. I'm not scared to fly; my anxiety comes from all that leads up to the flight and what comes after the flight. Getting to the airport on time, making sure I set the alarm correctly, packing for the trip, and finding the right gate are the things that really can raise my anxiety.

As we start to descend, my mind is whirling with how many bags we have, where my keys are, or how to find the rental car counter. I start looking through my purse for the confirmation numbers I will need long before we start to descend. I worry about long lines, when we will eat, where we will eat and whether we'll be able to find the kind of restaurant we like. I worry the hotel where we are booked is in an unsafe area. I worry they won't have our room ready or they won't have a room for us at all.

When we got off the plane in California, we had to get our luggage, find the shuttle bus to the car rental agency, rent the car and drive the California freeways to our hotel. I had printed directions off the internet to every possible destination for the whole weekend. What I didn't realize, however, was the directions I had printed to the hotel were from the airport, not the car rental location. I thought I could figure it out, but when we turned onto a main road, we were immediately faced with a freeway entrance. I made my best guess. My best guess was wrong. By the time I figured out we were going the wrong direction, it had begun to get dark. From the highway, I could not see the streets to the side. I finally got off the freeway, but now I was driving in an area that may or may not be extremely dangerous. Remember I was from Wisconsin and most of what I know about Los Angeles is from watching TV!

I called my husband and he was trying to help me navigate from internet maps 2,000 miles away. These were the days before smart phones with GPS. My anxiety was rising with each mile I drove. Finally I saw a gas station that looked safe. I saw other women with children around. We bought a good map and asked for directions. By now, my daughter and I were close to tears. We were hungry. We'd been hoping to have room service in the hotel for dinner. I was stressed and my daughter was definitely feeling it. Now we had gotten so far off course we had to drive straight through downtown LA to get to our destination. Even with a map, we still got turned around and had a hard time finding the hotel. It took us three hours to get from the airport to the hotel. It should have taken a half hour.

After a good night's sleep, we had a wonderful trip, but don't you know my daughter will never let me forget that terrible drive? When we trust in God and allow Him to lead us to the spacious place, we should be living in a place of peace, not anxiety. This week we will be looking at our anxieties, and our great and powerful God. We will study the life of David and work on realigning our perspectives together.

MEMORY VERSE:

> *Do not be anxious about anything, but in everything, by prayer and petition, with thanksgiving, present your requests to God. And the peace of God, which transcends all understanding, will guard your hearts and your minds in Christ Jesus.*
>
> ≈ *Philippians 4:6-7*

ක්‍ර Day 1 ක්‍ර

David

id you know Psalm 31 is not the only place David mentions the concept of the spacious place? Look up 2 Samuel 22:17-20. These verses are in the middle of a song of praise written by David. This song of praise is also included in the Bible in Psalm 18, with a few changes. The duplication indicates David's song of praise was probably used as a general hymn of thanksgiving. Read 2 Samuel 22:1 to get a little bit of background.

This week we are going to look at the life of our author, David, in order to understand what he meant when he said God set his feet in a spacious place.

Take a few minutes to glance through the chapters listed and fill in this chart. Feel free to use the headings in your Bible to remind you what happened in each story. I won't consider it cheating! If you are unfamiliar with these stories, I would encourage you to find some time to read through them more carefully. If you are short on time try to look at half of them. Think about what fears or anxieties David might have experienced in each situation.

Major event in David's life	Chapter reference	What type of anxiety or fear might this event have produced in David?
Samuel anointed David as the future king	1 Samuel 16	
David killed Goliath	1 Samuel 17	
Saul tried to kill David	1 Samuel 19	

David became king – inquired of God	2 Samuel 2 (especially verse 1)	
David brought the ark back to Jerusalem	2 Samuel 6 (especially verse 9)	
David wanted to build a temple for the Lord	2 Samuel 7	
David committed adultery with Bathsheba and had her husband murdered	2 Samuel 11	
David repented of his sin	2 Samuel 12	
One of David's children raped another of David's children	2 Samuel 13	
In revenge, another son killed the offending son	2 Samuel 13	
Another son of David's, Absalom, conspired against David and he fled.	2 Samuel 15	
David mourned Absalom's death	2 Samuel 18	

What is your overall reaction to this list? Did anything surprise you?

What are the general categories of fear or anxiety you see in the list?

Which of these fears or anxieties are also struggles for you? What situations are you facing that bring out these anxieties?

Let's end today reading part of David's song of praise again. After all that had happened in his life, this song is rich with meaning and true emotion. Below is 2 Samuel 22:17-20. Circle just one word that speaks to you of your personal situation. Tell God what it means to you.

He reached down from on high and took hold of me; he drew me

out of deep waters. He rescued me from my powerful enemy, from

my foes, who were too strong for me. They confronted me in the

day of my disaster, but the Lord was my support. He brought me

out into a spacious place; he rescued me because he delighted in me.

Response and/or prayer:

You have not handed me over to the enemy but have set my feet in a spacious place.

≈ **Day 2** ≈

The Cave and the Spacious Place

Our family recently visited some caves in the area where we now live in Missouri. Jesse James, the outlaw, supposedly hid out there in the late 1800s. These caves are huge and continue on room after room. The natural formations were lit and railings and stairs had been added to help visitors see the caves safely. At one point in the tour, the tour guide turned out the lights so we could see just how dark it is in the cave. It was pitch black and I could not see my hand in front of my face. We really enjoyed our visit to the caves, and our kids really felt adventurous. However, it felt great to leave! We walked out into the fresh air, felt the sunshine on our faces and saw the big sky above. Being in a cave can be fun for a time, but the enclosed spaces would get to me after a while. Maybe one of the reasons David used the image of the spacious place is because he spent so much time hiding in caves.

In 1 Samuel 24, David and his men have to flee from Saul who was trying to kill David. David is hiding in a cave in the Desert of En Gedi near the Crags of the Wild Goats. Sounds like the name of some wonderful exotic spa, doesn't it? Not quite!

Read 1 Samuel 24. Let's establish a few facts:

How many men did David have (1 Samuel 23:13)?

How many men did Saul have (1 Samuel 24:2)?

Fair fight? Hardly. **What do verses 5 and 6 tell you about David's character and the types of worries he might have had?**

You have not handed me over to the enemy but have set my feet in a spacious place.

Why does David spare Saul's life?

Imagine yourself an observer as David came out and showed himself to Saul. What other outcomes could there have been?

Do you think David trusts Saul or does he trust God as he lays himself prostrate before Saul? Why do you think he does this?

Look at Saul's response. He clearly realized David spared his life. What does verse 21 tell you about Saul's trust in David? Does he anticipate a peaceful outcome of this encounter?

Did David trust Saul's change of heart? What is his next step?

The reason I want us to spend time in these stories is for us to really feel what David might have been feeling. He is a hunted man. All the odds are against him. The result of the episode we looked at today could have been his death, Saul's death, or a bloody battle between two groups of warriors. David could have also stayed in the cave, remained hidden and Saul would never have been the wiser.

All of this provides insight into the prayers or songs of David as he reflects back on his life. Perhaps David was thinking of this moment in particular when he wrote Psalm 31:8. If you can, write it here from memory.

The same great God who saved David from his enemy Saul is powerful enough to save you from the enemies you face. Look back on week 1, day 5. That day we talked about enemies we face. **Is there one major enemy you are facing right now?**

You have not handed me over to the enemy but have set my feet in a spacious place.

Tomorrow we will be focusing on how powerful our God is and how He desires to save us from our enemies.

Response and/or prayer:

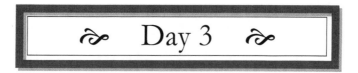

∾ Day 3 ∾

Trusting our Great God

After all David had been through, he still praised God. Second Samuel 22 is evidence of David's talent, creativity, and amazing way with word pictures. Let's break down the hymn and see what we can learn about the God who can save us from our enemies and bring us into a spacious place.

Read 2 Samuel 22:1-7. What can you learn about God from these verses?

Read 2 Samuel 22:8-20. What can you learn about God from these verses?

Read 2 Samuel 22:21-25. (Some commentators think these verses were written before David's sin with Bathsheba. Others believe they refer to his faithfulness to God when he was king, and not his failures in his personal life.) What can you learn about God from these verses?

You have not handed me over to the enemy but have set my feet in a spacious place.

Read 2 Samuel 22:26-37. What can you learn about God from these verses?

Read 2 Samuel 22:38-46. What can you learn about God from these verses?

Read 2 Samuel 22:47-51. What can you learn about God from these verses?

Glance back on what you learned about God today. Listen to the Holy Spirit. Is He prompting you to focus on a particular attribute of God today?

We all want to be in the spacious place, I think. We all desire to release our anxieties and live a life full of peace and rest. However, the reality of living that out day to day is harder than it seems. One key to releasing anxieties is to trust the power of our great God. The key to building that trust is being constantly aware of His ability to handle our situation. It's easy to say, "You just need to trust God!" But, you would be a fool to trust God if He wasn't powerful enough to help you.

To live in peace, we need to trust God.
To trust God, we need to know God.

Do you remember the song *God is an Awesome God?* One line in the song talks about how God reigns with wisdom, power and love. When I was pregnant with our third child, my husband was faced with a job situation. The company where he worked was closing the local office and wanted him to move to another city. We didn't want to move so he was scrambling to find another job. We had people around us who loved us like crazy, but they lacked wisdom because they didn't understand his field and they lacked the power to provide him with a job. We knew people who were powerful, but they lacked love for us and wisdom to know what would be best for our family. We knew people who were extremely wise but had no connections that would help us get him a new job and who didn't know us enough to love us. The only one to turn to was God. He had the wisdom to know what was best for us. He had the power to make it happen. He loved us enough to desire the best for us. In the end he provided an amazing job fitting my husband's skills, personality, and experience in ways we could not have imagined. We also got insurance in place in time for the baby's birth. Our God truly is an awesome God.

It's easy to look back on that time and see God's hand and see how trustworthy He is. However, at the time I was full of anxiety and worry.

If you are in the middle of a situation that is filling you with anxiety, how can you get to know God better, trust Him more, and experience His peace more fully?

You have not handed me over to the enemy but have set my feet in a spacious place.

Response and/ or prayer:

Peace

As I write this Bible study, I have a deep concern for one of my children. The concern regards her mental and physical health. I'm struggling to feel peace about the situation. I'm working hard to keep my anxieties in check. If I allowed myself to think ahead to the possibilities, the worst case scenarios, I'd curl up in a ball and never get out of bed again. Instead, I'm working hard to think one step at a time. What do I need to do today to help her? What should the next step be?

I sat in the waiting room of the doctor's office yesterday fighting tears. The desire to wallow in self-pity was strong. I thought about people I could call to ask for prayer. I thought about books I should get and read or other families who had been through this whom I could talk to. I imagined what other people would think about us as a parents if this problem ended up exploding into a more serious situation. I thought of the ways I had failed as a mother; how I was to blame. The last thought I had was to be still and pray. This is so often the case for me.

Trusting God with this situation is so hard for me and is a process I have not yet conquered. Reminding myself of His power and love for me helps. Living in the spacious place in the midst of a situation like this takes daily commitment.

What are your top three worries?

1.

2.

3.

Now think for a moment about what it would look like to have peace in each of these areas. Describe how it would feel. How would your behavior change.

1.

You have not handed me over to the enemy but have set my feet in a spacious place.

2.

3.

If you, like me, are also experiencing an anxiety causing time in your life, consider adopting Psalm 23 as a daily reading. You may already know it by heart. Write it in your own handwriting in the space below.

On what characteristics of God is David relying in this psalm?
Read slowly, verse by verse and think about what David believes about
God.

Which of these characteristics is hardest for you to accept? Why?

I struggle to accept my cup overflows when I feel my life is hard, or not
all it could be. I look at other families and other women and find myself
jealous. I focus on the world around me, and all the advertisements
bombarding us every day, and I see things I do not have. I too often focus
on the world around me and not on the heavenly father who graciously and
lovingly provides me with everything I could possibly need.

One observation I have made lately about my anxieties is they are
accompanied by physical tension. My back gets stiff. My shoulders and neck
tense up. I grind my teeth at night and sometimes catch myself gritting
them during the day.

Can you think of any physical symptoms that accompany worry and

You have not handed me over to the enemy but have set my feet in a spacious place.

anxiety for you?

I'm trying to teach myself to use these symptoms as clues I am allowing anxiety to creep in and I'm not enjoying the promise of the spacious place. When I notice the physical tension, I take a deep breath and stretch my neck a bit. I try to relax my muscles while I acknowledge the tension to God. Then I pray a quick prayer and picture my spacious place. This refocuses me from my worries back to God and to the great gift of peace He has for me.

What truth could you remind yourself this week when you notice tension and anxiety creeping in?

Response and/or prayer:

Casting Your Cares on Him

Today we are going to look at some passages on anxieties and worries. Let's see what we can learn and pray we can allow it to change our lives.

Read the following verses slowly, then answer the questions that follow.

Psalm 55:22

Cast your cares on the Lord and he will sustain you; he will never let the righteous fall.

Proverbs 12:25

An anxious heart weighs a man down, but a kind word cheers him up.

Matthew 6:25

Therefore I tell you, do not worry about your life, what you will eat or drink; or about your body, what you will wear. Is not life more important than food, and the body more important than clothes? Look at the birds of the air; they do not sow or reap or store away in barns, and yet your heavenly Father feeds them. Are you not much more valuable than they? Who of you by worrying can add a single hour to his life?

Philippians 4:6-7

You have not handed me over to the enemy but have set my feet in a spacious place.

Do not be anxious about anything, but in everything, by prayer and petition with thanksgiving, present your requests to God. And the peace of God, which transcends all understanding, will guard your hearts and your minds in Christ Jesus.

1 Peter 5:7

Cast all your anxiety on him because he cares for you.

What do these verses say about what worry can do to us? In your experience have you found this to be true? When?

What do these verses say about what those who choose to follow Christ should do with their worries and anxieties?

In your experience how hard or easy is that to do? Why?

What do these verses say will be the result if you follow their advice? What promises are there for us?

Why does God want us to cast our anxieties on Him?

What is the Holy Spirit wanting to teach you today? What one insight from today is making you stop and think?

In *The Ragamuffin Gospel*, Brennan Manning says, "In essence, there is only one thing God asks of us – that we be men and women of prayer, people who live close to God, people for whom God is everything and for whom God is enough. That is the root of peace."

What is your reaction to this quote? Do you see how understanding this could help you live a more peaceful life? How?

As we close out another week, spend some time in prayer today talking

You have not handed me over to the enemy but have set my feet in a spacious place.

to Him about what you are learning about the spacious place.

Response and/ or prayer:

WEEK 4: ACCEPTANCE NOT JUDGMENT

After my third child was born I decided to start running to lose the last of the baby weight. You have to understand I was not an athlete as a kid. In fact I had never run a mile without walking. When we ran the mile in high school gym class, I finished dead last and the coach looked worried and concerned at my beet red face. So for me to pick up running was pretty extraordinary. I started slowly and worked up to three miles. I ran my first 5k race and was so proud of myself. Ultimately I ran several 5ks, several 10ks and some 5 mile races as well.

As I was lining up before a 5 mile race, I recognized a woman I knew. I hadn't known she was a runner. We chatted for a few minutes. When I mentioned the speed at which I had been training (a slow pace), she said how great it was I had trained for the race. She hadn't been training at all. So here she was, just showing up to run 5 miles. I on the other hand had taken months to train for this event.

This conversation completely deflated me. All the hard work, all the mini-goals I had set and reached, how pleased and proud of myself I had been, were all floating away in that early morning sky. Now, please know this woman had no idea. She had no intention of insulting me, or trying to impress me with her accomplishments. I was the one being judgmental. As she walked away, I was the one beating myself up, allowing discouragement to set in. I was the one who decided my accomplishments weren't good enough. I was the one who called myself a failure.

The spacious place is a place of acceptance, not judgment. I think we've all felt judgment from others. It's a common human experience. Some of us, though, also get judgment from ourselves, and that can be the harshest judgment of all. This week, we are going to spend some time in Luke 13 with Jesus and a woman he healed. My prayer is you can finish this week knowing how to live in the knowledge Jesus has accepted you and He calls you His Beloved.

MEMORY VERSE:

> *This then is how we know that we belong to the truth, and how we set our hearts at rest in his presence whenever our hearts condemn us. For God is greater than our hearts, and he knows everything.*

> ☙ *1 John 3:19-20*

The Crippled Woman

In Luke 13, Jesus has an incredible interaction with a woman who had been suffering with a physical ailment for years. Let's dig into the passage and see what we can learn.

Read Luke 13:10-17.

Let's start with the woman. What was causing her suffering? How long had she dealt with this?

Because of her disability, what direction was she forced to look?

She showed up to where Jesus was teaching. What does it tell you about her attitude toward Jesus? How she might have been feeling about her situation?

Luke's choice to include this story here is interesting. Look back a couple of chapters, noticing the headings. Look forward a couple of chapters. What comes before the story and after this story in Luke's gospel?

Let's think about that for a second. Luke is in the middle of recording the teachings of Jesus, His parables, encouragements and warnings. Yet he stops to tell this story of the healing of a crippled woman.

Why do you think Luke records this here? What can we learn from this story's placement in scripture?

Now let's look at what Jesus does. What does Luke tell us Jesus did *first?*

Considering she was in a large crowd, and bent over from her ailment, how easy would it have been for Jesus to see her?

What action is recorded next?

What was Jesus doing when He saw her and called her over (verse 10)?

Write the words Jesus spoke to the woman here:

When I taught school, I spent a couple of years teaching in a Jewish Yeshiva. The kids spent half their days receiving religious training from rabbis and then secular classes were taught during the other half of the day by teachers from any religion. The school was in an orthodox area and most of the families at the school lived by a strict set of rules. One of the first instructions I was given by my principal was the men and women never touched. Even accidental touching would require a man to perform a ceremonial cleaning. As a teacher I had been in the habit of shaking hands with parents when I met them and this was a hard habit to unlearn! Men simply didn't touch women in the Jewish culture.

What did Jesus do according to verse 13?

Amazing! I wonder how much physical touch she had received in her life. I wonder if Jesus knew she needed to feel His touch, not just for the power it contained, but for the love it communicated. This isn't the only time Jesus chooses compassion over following rituals and laws.

What was the woman's immediate reaction?

What is her posture now? Where is she directing her gaze?

Read 2 Samuel 22:18-20 again, keeping in mind the story of the crippled woman in Luke 13. List ways her situation parallels this passage.

Knowing what you know so far about this story, do you think she was exhibiting the blessings and benefits of the spacious place? In what ways?

The woman didn't have a guarantee that coming to hear Jesus teach would result in her healing. She could have stayed home; perhaps she was in pain. She could have sought healing elsewhere. But she turned to Jesus.

When you are in pain or are suffering, where do you go? Do you seek out Jesus?

You have not handed me over to the enemy but have set my feet in a spacious place.

What could help you remember to turn to Him first?

What an awesome story! But it doesn't end there. Tomorrow we'll look at the response this interaction garnered.

Response and/or prayer:

The Accusers

Yesterday, in Luke 13:10-17, we saw how Jesus brought healing and joy to a woman who had been suffering for eighteen years. Her response to Jesus was just what God wants from us when we have been touched and healed by Christ. She praised God. Not everyone was so pleased at this turn of events. Let's look at what happened next.

What is the synagogue ruler's objection to this healing?

To whom did he address his concerns? Check those that apply:

- o Jesus
- o The woman who had been healed
- o The crowd
- o God, in prayer

What do you think that might indicate about the ruler's motives?

I think it is significant Jesus is not being directly blamed here. Yet He comes to the defense of this woman. She had been suffering for 18 years. She is healed and turns her praise heavenward. Then, immediately she is attacked for not doing it "right."

You have not handed me over to the enemy but have set my feet in a spacious place.

Summarize the argument Jesus used in the woman's defense.

How do you think the woman might have felt while Jesus reprimanded the synagogue ruler?

The Pharisees were constantly after Jesus during His ministry. What objections do they voice in each of these passages?

Luke 5:21

Luke 5:30

Luke 6:2

Luke 6:7

Luke7:39

Luke 11:38

What can you conclude about the Pharisees from these passages?

Have you ever felt accused or judged by someone? What happened? How did it feel?

It seems to me we humans have a tendency to make up rules as we go along. These rules are often of little concern to God. Two very human attitudes are at the root of this kind of rule-writing. One attitude is insecurity. When we are unsure what to do, then come to a decision, we can elevate that decision to have an importance it doesn't deserve. We want to be validated by having others make the same decision. If others join you in your choice, it makes you look "right."

The other attitude responsible for this seems to be its opposite. In reality, they are closely related. That attitude is arrogance. We cannot imagine why someone would make a different choice. We assume they must be wrong in order for us to be right.

What are some rules you have noticed people invent? The rules may be based on tradition, religion or trends.

You have not handed me over to the enemy but have set my feet in a spacious place.

Which, if any, of these rules are ones God would agree are essentials?

Are you holding yourself or others to a standard that is NOT from God?

The spacious place into which we are invited by God is a place of acceptance, not judgment. This woman was judged by the accusers, but accepted by Jesus. When we focus on the accusers around us and ignore the acceptance of Jesus, we are refusing His offer of the spacious place. Ask the Holy Spirit to examine your heart and show you where your blind spots might be in regards to judgement and acceptance.

Response and/or prayer:

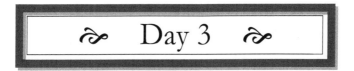

Daughter of Abraham

Today let's try to draw a few conclusions from the story we've been studying. I asked a couple of questions in the last two days about the direction of the woman's gaze in different parts of the story. I believe this to be key.

Before she was healed, her gaze was at the ground.

When she was accused by the synagogue ruler, she could have gotten stuck with her gaze on her accusers.

After she was healed, her gaze was at the sky, towards God in heaven.

Let's think about this for a moment. In my life, I often have my gaze stuck. Sometimes I'm stuck with my gaze on the ground. I'm so focused on the task before me, the to-do list, the mountain of laundry, the needs of my kids, my worries, the messages on my voice mail, the emails piling up, the cards that need to be sent, the presents that need to be bought, the birthday parties that need to be planned...I could go on for a long time! When we focus on our day to day life, it's like we are stuck looking at the ground.

Other times we get caught with our gaze on the accusers. All around us are people who are doing life differently from us. Some of them are doing it better. Their kids are better behaved, they make more money, their marriages look happier, they have accomplished more in life, they are never late or forget to sign permission slips. Others of them seem to be struggling more than we are. Their marriages seem less happy, their kids wear stained clothes, they are less accomplished, they forget to send their children's lunches to school.

There will always be someone doing life better than us, and there will always be someone doing life less successfully than us. So if we want to feel superior, we can. If we want to feel inferior, we can. When we get caught up in the comparison game, we are focusing on our accusers. Sometimes the accuser is someone else, looking down on us, but often, I think, the accuser is ourselves. We compare and contrast, feel elevated or deflated, feel vindicated or condemned.

Our example in Luke 13 however, gets caught up in none of this. What a wonderful example for us.

What does Luke 13:13 say she does "immediately?"

How cool is that? I want to grow up to be like the crippled woman. When I am overwhelmed with my situation, I want to seek out Jesus, the great healer. I want to let Him touch me. I want to immediately raise my gaze to God in praise.

In the book *Show Me the Way*, Henri Nouwen says, "When we cling to the results of our actions as our only way of self-identification, then we become possessive and defensive and tend to look at our fellow beings more as enemies to be kept at a distance than as friends with whom we share the gifts of life."

Based on your experiences in life, do you agree with this quote? Why or why not?

What does Jesus call the woman in verse 16? Why do you think this particular name would be significant in this setting?

We never learn the woman's actual name in this story, but we do know that Jesus named her. He drew her into the inner circle. He made her one of His children. He gave her equality with the synagogue ruler who claimed the sonship of Abraham as his key to God's kingdom. He gave her identity and significance. And that significance came from how she was related to Him.

Read verse 16 in the New Living Translation:

> This dear woman, a daughter of Abraham, has been held in
>
> bondage by Satan for eighteen years. Isn't it right that she be
>
> released even on the Sabbath?

My friend, Jesus wants to heal you too. He considers you dear, one of His. When our identity comes properly from Him, our gaze will lift from our day to day situation, pass the accusers, go heavenward and we will praise God.

Take a moment to think about where you are right now in your life. Where does your gaze most often rest? Why?

Whom do you consider to be the accusers in your life?

How would your feelings about your identity be different if you could direct your gaze more often toward God? What would pale in importance?

You have not handed me over to the enemy but have set my feet in a spacious place.

Ask God to help you as you think about the direction of your gaze today. Pay attention to what is heavy on your mind. Find reasons to direct your gaze to Him.

Response and/or prayer:

Judgment

I like lists. I like to be organized. I like to check items off my list, eventually crumpling it up and throwing it away with a dramatic flourish. I keep a detailed calendar and I hate missing appointments. I hate the feeling there is something I need to do today, but I can't remember what it is. If I get all my tasks done, make all my appointments, then everyone will see how good I am. No one can think poorly about me. For me, it's all about appearances.

I had developed a good habit that may be familiar to you. Each week I would list the roles I was filling that week (wife, mother, volunteer, employee, etc.) and I would set a goal for each one. Then I scheduled time to accomplish each goal. How efficient of me! However, I came to see my goals were based on how I looked to other people. I wanted other people to think I was a great homemaker, so I prioritized cleaning and organizing. I wanted other people to see how committed I was so I volunteered for more activities. I wanted other people to be impressed with my accomplishments so I spent too much time working on writing projects or work projects. I was too focused on accomplishment.

This is what it is like to live under judgment. For me, it was being constantly busy, trying to keep the internal and external accusers at bay. Instead of rejecting what the accusers were saying, I bought into it and kept trying harder to fit the mold.

What are some of the messages you have heard from the accusers in your life (others and yourself)?

Look at your list and put a star by the messages you bought into even if for just a short time.

You have not handed me over to the enemy but have set my feet in a spacious place.

What can you conclude about your own propensity to keep your gaze on the accusers from your answers?

If you have been able to reject some of these messages from the accusers, how did you reject them? What helped you see truth?

If you are a person who hasn't been able to get beyond the voices of the accusers, why do you think that is?

I'd like to give you a few scriptures which may help you in the future as you encounter accusers and are tempted to set your gaze on them.

Look up each verse and summarize it in your own words:

Isaiah 43:1

Galatians 2:6

Hebrews 4:16

God calls you by name. If you have made the decision to follow Christ, to allow Him to be the Lord of your life, you belong to Him. Those others that seem important pale in comparison with our great God. When we need Him, we can be confident in approaching the throne of God Himself and He will provide us with mercy and grace.

My habit of setting priorities and goals with the roles and goals method was good, but it needed some tweaking. At the suggestion of a wise friend, I decided to change my habit. The old way was reinforcing my wrong priorities. Instead of setting roles and goals, I decided to start setting relationship goals. I listed the six most important relationships in my life (God, my husband, my three children, and myself). Then I chose one thing I needed to do that week to show my love for them. I included myself because I also needed to take care of myself, exercise, eat well, and find time to write and relax. Sometimes I have to ask my husband or a child what I can do for them that week. I've never had a negative response to that question!

This change has dramatically changed what I do week to week. For me it has helped me keep the accusers from determining my actions. Some items would have been pushed to the bottom of the old list are now top priorities. For example, my son has been wanting to write a book this summer. He talked about it a lot, but didn't know where to start. So I scheduled time to sit down with him and get an outline planned. The time we spent together on this project was so precious. He must have hugged me every five minutes while we worked. Meanwhile, my house is a disaster. I haven't planted any flowers in my yard or pulled any weeks. I want to do some home decorating projects like sewing curtains, but that will have to wait. Of course, the book project never got finished, but that wasn't really the point.

This works for me because I like lists and they help me. For some of you a list is just another accuser, pointing out your faults and failings. The last thing I want to do is be another accuser in your life pointing out ways that you don't measure up.

You have not handed me over to the enemy but have set my feet in a spacious place.

Consider how you spend your time and prioritize your obligations. Are there changes that need to be made? Pray for guidance and wisdom.

Response and/or prayer:

Acceptance

I once knew a man who was interested in becoming "religious" but was held back by one thing. He said he would have to change too much before he could turn to God. I imagine he felt his lifestyle was too different from Christians he knew. He would have to clean up his act before he could come to church or start thinking about religion. How unfortunate he bought into that lie. And shame on us, the people of God, for having a history of judgment. The spacious place is a place of acceptance, not judgment, no matter where you are on your journey toward God.

The woman we have been studying this week came to God as she was. She wasn't presentable, perfect or without flaw. To be a person who accepts God's gift of the spacious place, we do not have to be perfect. The spacious place is earthly, it is not heaven. Heaven is a place without sin, a holy and perfect place. That will only exist for us when this life is over. Let me try to be clear about the spacious place. The spacious place is not just positive thinking. It is not just focusing on your "happy place." It is not an attitude we can adopt by sheer will. It is not being a cheery, perpetually optimistic person who ignores the bad in the world.

**The spacious place is not a state of mind,
it is a state of relationship.**

I believe the spacious place is a state of relationship with God. When David used this idea to express what God had done in his life, he saw that God removed him from his enemies and provided for him this place of calm and rest in the midst of his crazy life. And yet so many of us stay in the place of our enemies, ignoring the place of relationship God is offering to us. We do not have to make ourselves perfect before we can enjoy the spacious place. The spacious place is about our relationship with God. We can come to Him before we are perfected. He accepts us as we are and desires us to come to Him.

I have often thought in some way God is easier to please than the world. Isn't that interesting? The world thinks of itself as extremely accepting. The world says, "anything goes." And yet, the world also demands perfection in how we look, how we act, how we think. Just look at the women on the cover of magazines who are stunningly beautiful and yet have to be airbrushed and digitally altered. Think about how the world reacts when we express an idea they don't consider "tolerant" enough.

The world also thinks God is the one who is judgmental, the one who demands perfection. They see God as a tyrant, demanding money and devotion from His followers. But God is the one who takes us as we are, where we are, and loves us unconditionally.

Some of us have bought into the world's idea God is judgmental and the world is accepting. That's upside down and backward.

In what ways have you seen the world's claim that it is accepting? In what ways have you seen the world is, in reality, quite judgmental?

Have you ever bought into the lie that God is judgmental? How?

Has God shown Himself to be accepting in your life? Consider where you may have missed His love and acceptance for you.

Think of someone you know who lives as if judged everyday by God. Without naming names, describe how it affects a person's life.

Do you know someone who lives life knowing they are accepted by God? What does it look like?

Where do you think you fall in that spectrum? Put an x where you see yourself:

I fully understand I am accepted by God		I feel judged daily by God

I've noticed in my own life many of the messages I think are from God regarding what I "should" do or "ought" to have done are not from God. When you learn to hear the voice of the Holy Spirit, you will see it is not harsh. His voice is not full of recriminations. He is not constantly fed up with you.

Copy Romans 8:1 below:

Read John 3:17. What does it say about God's attitude towards us?

You have not handed me over to the enemy but have set my feet in a spacious place.

Switch to the end of the New Testament to read 1 John 3:19-20. Whom do these verses say condemns us? (I realize this looks like a mistake flipping from John to 1 John since the references are so similar!)

According to the previous verse (1 John 3:18), how do we rest in His presence?

I'd like to end this week with this passage, Isaiah 28:10-13.

> For it is:
>
> Do and do, do and do,
>
> rule on rule, rule on rule;
>
> a little here, a little there.
>
> Very well then, with foreign lips and strange tongues
>
> God will speak to his people,

to whom he said,

"This is the resting place, let the weary rest",

and, "This is the place of repose" –

but they would not listen.

So then the word of the Lord to them will become:

Do and do, do and do,

rule on rule, rule on rule;

a little here, a little there –

so that they will go and fall backward,

be injured and snared and captured.

Are you so busy doing, following rules, and doing some more that you are not hearing God offer you a place of repose, a resting place?

Talk to God today about whether you feel accepted or judged. Spend some time quietly listening to God. Consider memorizing Romans 8:1.

Response and/or prayer:

WEEK 5: PROTECTION NOT ABANDONMENT

This spring we had the most amazing view out our kitchen window. A robin was busy building a nest in the tree. For weeks we watched her fly back and forth, finding twigs, stems, and soft nesting materials. She wove them together expertly. Occasionally, she would spread herself out and wiggle back and forth to form the nest to the shape of her body. Eventually, she was done and we noticed her sitting in the nest constantly. All this time, we noticed another robin. He was usually close to the road, standing on the lawn or the driveway. It was as if he was guarding the nest and his family. Finally, we saw tiny little beaks sticking up above the rim of the nest. Baby birds are so ugly they are cute!

Then we noticed it wasn't just the mama bird who was gathering food for her babies. The papa bird was also catching bugs and worms bringing them back to the nest. It was the best dinnertime entertainment we've ever had as a family. I found myself choking up thinking about how well these birds were caring for their young. On a field trip for my son's fourth grade class, I asked a bird expert about the papa bird and he confirmed they do in fact guard the nest and family.

What an amazing picture of protection God has woven into the instincts of this little animal. Likewise, God is our protector and He will never abandon us. Understanding the idea of the spacious place means knowing we are protected by God and not abandoned by Him no matter what the circumstances of our lives are.

This week we are going back in time, predating the psalm written by David, to study Joseph. If any Bible character has the right to feel abandoned by God, Joseph certainly did. And yet, God never lifted His protection from Joseph. I can't wait to see what God has for us to learn this week.

MEMORY VERSE:

But God sent me ahead of you to preserve for you a remnant on earth and to save your lives by a great deliverance. So then, it was not you who sent me here, but God.

Genesis 45:7-8a

Joseph

When I was ten years old or so, I came home from school one day at noon because we had a half-day. The plan was I would let myself in the house with the hidden key and make myself lunch. I felt so proud and excited to be allowed this new freedom and responsibility. But when I got home, the hidden key was not where it was supposed to be. I was locked out of the house with no lunch. I can remember the feeling of abandonment so clearly, even today. Were you ever lost when you were a child? Was you name ever spoken over the loud speakers at K-Mart or the grocery store? The opportunities to feel abandoned as an adult can be even more acute.

We can feel alone, abandoned, exposed or betrayed. When the circumstances in our lives lead us to have these feelings, it is understandable we might assume God has removed His presence from us. We think if He loves us so much, why would He allow these things to happen to us? I wonder if Joseph ever felt that way.

Read Genesis 37. (Remember Israel and Jacob are the same person.)

How would you describe the dynamics in the family?

Which character(s) do you think is or are to blame for the dynamics in this family?

You have not handed me over to the enemy but have set my feet in a spacious place.

This story is told in a fairly straightforward, factual way. Let's think about what the characters were probably feeling throughout the events in the story. List as many emotions as you can think of that they might have experienced.

In what way might have each of these characters in the story felt abandoned?

Joseph

Rueben

Other brothers

Jacob

Read the next part of the story in Genesis 39.

What evidence shows us the state of Joseph's relationship with God and this point in his life? In other words, has Joseph turned his back on God?

What does each of the following verses say about where God is at this point in Joseph's life?

Genesis 39:2

Genesis 39:3

Genesis 39:5

Genesis 39:20b-21

Genesis 39:23

Put yourself in Joseph's position. Would you have felt God's presence with you through these kinds of circumstances? Which of the difficulties Joseph faced would have been the hardest for you?

The text makes it clear Joseph's success is the result of the Lord's presence and blessing. Knowing that, as a young man, Joseph tended toward arrogance, what temptation would Joseph have faced as he continued to have success in life?

Joseph was in a tough position for many different reasons. He had been parented in such a way that the animosity between his brothers and himself had become violent. He had been physically attacked by his brothers, then abandoned by them in a way that placed him in danger for the rest of his life. His status went from favored son to slave in a foreign country. He is unjustly accused and imprisoned. How easy it would have been for Joseph to feel abandoned by God. How easy it would have been for him to turn his back on God in this foreign land and worship their gods.

Knowing what you know so far about the spacious place as a state of relationship with God, do you think Joseph could have been accepting the gift of the spacious place while experiencing what he did? What evidence do you see of that?

Tomorrow we'll continue with Joseph's story. For today think about your own life, your own troubles and difficulties. Honestly address this question with God: How present do you feel God is in the midst of your current circumstances?

Response and/or prayer:

ꙮ Day 2 ꙮ

Joseph, the Sequel

What an amazing contradiction it is that while Joseph was physically imprisoned by the Egyptians, God was with him, blessing him, showing him kindness, and granting him favor with the guards. How amazing that through it all, Joseph continued to worship God. I believe Joseph was able to enjoy the blessings of the spacious place even when his physical situation was the most oppressive.

Let's continue the story by reading Genesis 40.

What can you conclude about Pharaoh from this chapter?

Look carefully at Joseph's behavior and interactions. Can you tell anything about his state of mind or character at this point in his life?

Considering what the last verse of chapter 40 and the first verse of chapter 41 tell us, I imagine Joseph could have been feeling abandoned. The cupbearer forgets him and Joseph continues to live in a dungeon, punished for a crime he did not commit. As chapter 41 starts, Joseph had been in prison an additional two years. Read chapter 41.

Let's back up a little bit. Why were the cupbearer and the baker imprisoned? (Genesis 40:1)

And what was the fate of the chief baker?

So, Pharaoh was not a man to be approached without caution. Joseph had bad news to give Pharaoh. How frightening that could have been. What is your impression of Joseph as he speaks to Pharaoh and interprets his dream?

Joseph refers to God continually as he speaks to Pharaoh and even as he names his children. **What do these statements from Genesis reveal about Joseph's beliefs about God?**

41:16

41:25

41:28

41:32

41:51

41:52

One day Joseph is a prisoner, then next he is put in charge of the whole land of Egypt. Make a list of what life was like for him before and after this encounter with Pharaoh.

Before	After

When studying scripture, we can apply it in two ways. First, we can think about and choose a way to **act** differently based on the truth we are studying. Second, we can consider where our thinking may need to be adjusted and choose to **think** differently based on the truth we are studying. Ultimately changing the way we think about God will result in changing how we act. Both are important, but we can see how Joseph's theology (what he believed was true about God) impacted his daily life and actions. **Complete the following sentences with truths about God.**

When I am facing a difficult situation, God is…

When I don't see God's hand or presence, God is…

101

When I am afraid, God is…

When I see or experience injustice, God is…

No matter what I am feeling or experiencing, God is…

Response and/or prayer:

❧ Day 3 ❧

Family Reunion

The next several chapters of Genesis describing Joseph's reunion with his brothers are filled with powerful emotion and conflicting feelings. Joseph doesn't seem to know what to do with his brothers. Surely a desire for justice after all those years would have weighed heavily on his heart. At the same time he has been alone in a foreign land for so many years and here are his brothers before him. If you have the time today, read Genesis 42-44. If you are running tight on time, pick up the story in chapter 45.

In chapters 42-44, the brothers and Joseph interact but Joseph doesn't reveal his identity to them. What reasons can you think of that Joseph might have had for this?

The text repeatedly tells us Joseph weeps. (42:24, 43:30. 45:1-2) Why do you think this is emphasized?

A considerable amount of time passes between the first visit of the brothers and the second visit. How might this have helped Joseph?

By the time Joseph reveals his true identity, he has come to some conclusions about what God was doing in the situation. What is God's plan according to Joseph? (Genesis 45:4-8)

Was this conclusion about God's plan an easy assumption for Joseph or a difficult conclusion he came to over time? What evidence in the text do you see to support your answer?

This was no easy time for Joseph. He didn't just put on a happy face and say, "It is all in God's hands, whatever happens to me doesn't matter." He didn't ignore the wrongs that had been committed against him. This was an extremely difficult season for Joseph. All the pain, anger and betrayal must have rushed back in seeing the faces of his brothers. In the interactions between Joseph and his brothers we see a man deeply conflicted. God gave him time to process. Then, in the end, he was able to see clearly God had not abandoned him in these situations, but had used them to save an entire race of people. What amazing understanding Joseph was given.

Who sent Joseph to Egypt? (45:5, 8)

You have not handed me over to the enemy but have set my feet in a spacious place.

Notice Joseph's main concern in 45:5. Who is the object of his concern? Why?

Let's skip ahead a bit. Read Genesis 47:28. How long after the family settled in Egypt did Joseph's father Jacob live?

Read Genesis 50:15-21. It seems as if the brothers had been forgiven when Joseph first revealed his identity to them. However, years later, they are still waiting for retribution. Why do you think Joseph wept?

How is Joseph's approach to the difficult situations different from the approach of his brothers? Consider the whole story.

Genesis 50:24-25 reveals some of Joseph's final thought and requests. What do they reveal about Joseph's faith and beliefs?

Consider one quality of Joseph's character you admire. Is this a quality that is needed in your life? Think of one change you can make this week that would move you in the right direction.

Response and/or prayer:

You have not handed me over to the enemy but have set my feet in a spacious place.

  Day 4

Traffic Reports

We recently moved from a smaller sized town to a bigger city. In our smaller town we would complain about the "traffic" if we had to go slower than the speed limit. We would avoid the main highway when we could because of the "traffic." I put traffic in quotes because we really didn't know traffic until we moved to a bigger city. It is a whole different animal here. If the traffic is still moving at all, we are doing well. I still find myself avoiding freeways, but even the side streets can be congested. In our smaller town traffic helicopters were not necessary, but in the larger city we see traffic helicopters on a regular basis.

When you are stuck in traffic you have a limited view. You only know how fast the traffic around you is moving. I usually turn on the radio to see if I can get some more information. My hope is the traffic helicopter can see the whole maze of highways and let me know if an accident is ahead. The view from the traffic helicopter has the advantage of being able to see what is ahead and behind you. It can see where you are coming from and where you are headed.

Two views can be taken when looking at your life, and Joseph had two choices when it came to viewing his circumstances. He could have taken a ground level view. Or he could have taken an overhead view of his life. Both views have merit and both views can be misused.

On the negative side, ground level views can lead to misunderstanding the situations we are experiencing.

Some people call this navel-gazing or missing the forest for the trees. When we are too focused on the immediate circumstances around us, we can miss the bigger picture.

Consider a particular moment from Joseph's life. Remember when the cupbearer was released from prison? Joseph might have been optimistic about his chances for getting out of prison and getting justice. As he realized he was forgotten, what could he have been thinking if he had a ground level view?

What would he have missed if he had held that view.

On the positive side, overhead views give us perspective on our situation and remind us of God's promises and our ultimate destination, heaven.

Look back at Genesis 45:4-8 again. This is a great example of Joseph taking an overhead view. What would it have looked like if he took a ground level view at this point?

How do you think Joseph came to be a person who could so clearly see God's plan for him and for others? (This is purely conjectures. What do you think it takes to be that kind of a person?)

On the positive side, ground level views can help us develop sympathy and compassion for the hurts of people in difficult situations.

It's important not to discount ground level views altogether. Ground level views have some advantages as long as they are taken along with an overhead view. When we acknowledge what it feels like to go through trials in life, we allow ourselves and others to grieve, or be hurt, or to process our feelings. We wouldn't expect a woman who just became a widow to take an overhead view and not experience grief. The grief is just part of life, a part of the process.

In the passage we just read (45:4-8), Joseph reveals he's been thinking about what the brothers might be feeling or what worries they may have. What did he tell them not to do?

What does Ecclesiastes 3:4 acknowledge?

Even Jesus took time to mourn the loss of His friend Lazarus. He was grieving for the pain around Him, acknowledging what they were feeling. Read John 11:33-36. What was the reaction of Jesus to the weeping around Him?

If it was wrong to have a ground level view, what would His reaction have been?

On the negative side, overhead views can sometimes lead us to disregard or minimize the pain we or others go through in the day to day of life.

Have you ever experienced a time when your own pain was disregarded or minimized? What happened?

If a friend was going through a similar situation, how would you hope he or she would be treated?

At what point do you think it is appropriate to encourage an overhead view for a person in the middle of a terrible trial?

You have not handed me over to the enemy but have set my feet in a spacious place.

Is there some pain in your own life that you have not allowed yourself to feel? We don't want to dwell forever in the ground level view, but perhaps there is a time and place to allow yourself to feel pain. What is your reaction to this? Take your thoughts to the Lord.

Response and/or prayer:

∂ Day 5 *∂*

Whose story?

I have I've loved studying Joseph with you this week. Every time I dig into his story I come away with a renewed awe at the relationship Joseph must have had with God. The wisdom and perspective God gave Joseph is amazing. We too can have that kind of relationship with God. We are all parts of His story.

Does your Bible have a heading of some kind above the start of Genesis 37? If so write it here:

My Bible says "The Story of Joseph (37:1-50:26)."

Now write the first words of Genesis 37:2.

How interesting! Jacob is missing in much of the story of his son, Joseph. In what ways is this story Jacob's story?

We have the advantage of knowing the whole story all the way through modern times. When Joseph was being dragged to Egypt, or harassed by Potiphar's wife, or sitting in a dungeon, would Joseph have considered this

Jacob's story?

This story is Jacob's story in that it is much bigger than just the individual events in Joseph's life. The focus is not on him as a slave, or as a prisoner, or as an injured party in a family dispute. Joseph's story is about saving a nation of people from destruction. Joseph wasn't defined by his problems and we shouldn't be either. We are not just widows, abuse survivors, the sick, the wronged, the hurting, or the victims. The trials we face do not have to define our lives or our value. Our story is bigger than the events in our lives. We are part of something amazing, something God has been planning since before time began.

Yesterday we acknowledged there is a time for being in the present and looking at life from the ground level. However, staying there is not God's hope for us. We have been given the Bible and therefore we can see God's hand working generation to generation, age to age.

How can we achieve a heavenly view? Look at the following verses for habits and attitudes we can adopt to help us do this well.

Hebrews 12:2

Colossians 3:1-3

Matthew 6:19-21

Philippians 3:17-21

Philippians 4:8

Romans 12:2

2 Corinthians 4:16-18

Look over your answers. Does anything strike you or surprise you? What conclusions can you draw?

How difficult is it for you to keep an overhead view or a heavenly perspective? Which life events are most challenging for you? These can be real things that have happened or things you worry about. Offer them to God today.

After studying Joseph's story (actually Jacob's story!) this week, what truth can you claim regarding whether you are abandoned or protected in your day to day life?

You have not handed me over to the enemy but have set my feet in a spacious place.

The spacious place is ours when we lean on the promise that God protects us, and does not abandon us. Our lives will not be free from trouble. Joseph's life sure wasn't! But whatever we experience, God is there. He has not abandoned you. This is true when life is going well and when life seems to be crumbling around us. This is true when we feel it and when we don't. This is true. This is truth!

Response and/or prayer:

INTERMISSION

I must take a break here to explain to you the journey I've been on in writing this Bible study. The previous chapters, the introduction, the outline and the concepts were all written in 2010. I was really enjoying the process of researching, studying and creating this Bible study. Then my computer crashed and I had foolishly not backed it up. I did have a hard copy of most of the chapters. I had already written chapter 6 (next week's about Paul) but hadn't printed it out yet. So in my discouragement, I decided to shelve the project for a while.

It is now 2014 and I have decided to finish and get this out there, knowing it may fall like a lead balloon. The past four years have been difficult for me and my family. You may remember in week 3, day 4 I mentioned a deep concern I had for one of my children. That situation did not go away, it got worse. Some of those worst case scenarios I was allowing myself to contemplate came true. The path we found ourselves on was rocky and frightening. It shook my very foundations and threw everything I knew to be true into question. We are now on the other side of many of the struggles and the Lord has shown Himself to be unwaveringly faithful. I am choosing not to share very many details because this story isn't just my own and I want to be cautious and respectful of the feelings of my family members.

I say all this not to get sympathy from you. But I am at a different place spiritually writing the rest of this study. My faith was tested and I have been refined by fire. I had to step way back from trying to control my life and the lives of my children. God took us on a path I would never in a million years have chosen. All along the way He has made His involvement clear to us. We could see the working out of details, the orchestrating of people and events that could be nothing but the work of the Almighty.

I want you to know that these concepts I am writing about are not things I have conquered. I don't always live in freedom or peace. I struggle just like all of you do as you experience pain and heartache. If you feel like you don't have life all figured out, join the club. It is my prayer this will be a tool of growth for you. Dig in to the last few weeks of the study, praying for God to speak to you. I believe the Lord can use anything to sanctify us, even the words of a broken woman like myself.

WEEK 6: TRUTH NOT LIES

So far we have learned that in the spacious place, God provides us with freedom, peace, acceptance and protection. He also provides for us the truth. In John 14:6 Jesus says, "I am the way, the truth and the life," but in John 8:44, Satan is called the "father of lies." Whose messages do we believe? This week we will study Paul's life and writings for clues about the truths we can accept and that can change our lives.

For many years my internal vocabulary was (and still is, if I'm honest) full of words like *must, have to, ought to, should have, can't, shouldn't have, if only,* and *either/or.* The sentences surrounding these words were often lies I was blindly accepting. One day when my oldest daughter was in preschool, I forgot to have her pick an item to bring for show and tell. Show and tell is a big deal when you are in preschool. I felt that familiar feeling, the discouragement of knowing I had forgotten yet one more thing. Thankfully, my minivan was a disgusting mess! We just looked around in all the toys and sippy cups and garbage in the car and found a little teddy bear for her to take into the school.

The feelings I struggled with went far beyond realizing I was disorganized that day. My internal voices were telling me I was *always* disorganized and I *should have* had it all together. They said *if only* I were smarter, less lazy, and paid more attention, I could be more like the moms with clean cars and thoughtful show and tell items. Even though we are now out of the show and tell stage, I still struggle with the message that I must be more organized, must be more on top of things and must work harder.

Beginning to live in the spacious place God has provided means I can let go of those lies and start to hear the truth of who I am according to God, my creator. Having a right view of who you are in Christ is an essential element of having a right relationship with the Father. Living in the spacious place gives us room to evaluate where we stand with Christ. Let's dig into the New Testament to uncover some of God's truths.

MEMORY VERSE:

Teach me your way, O lord, and I will walk in your truth; give me an undivided heart, that I may fear your name.

            ❧ *Psalm 86:11*

Paul

P aul was arguably the most influential of the apostles of Christ, shaping and forming early Christianity. Paul never met Jesus during His earthly life and ministry. Today we are going to look at Paul's conversion. Remember Paul's name is Saul in the beginning of his story.

Acts 7 records the words of Stephen when he came before the high priest in the Sanhedrin and had to answer to the charge of blasphemy. He gives an amazing summary of God's work among his people starting with Abraham, Moses, and Joshua and ending with Solomon. Read the final words of his speech in Acts 7:51-53.

Who does Stephen accuse? (see Acts 7:1)

What is Stephen's accusation?

Read the rest of chapter 7 and 8:1. What role did Paul play in the stoning of Stephen?

You have not handed me over to the enemy but have set my feet in a spacious place.

Read Acts 8:3, and 9:1-19. What can we learn about Paul's personality from these passages?

What does Ananias' reaction to the Lord's request reveal about Paul?

Read Acts 22:6-21. This is Paul's account of the same events in his own words. In this account, Paul tells us what Ananias said to him. **Think about Ananias' role. What might he have been thinking and feeling?**

God is amazing in that nothing in Paul's background was wasted. Every bit of Paul's education, citizenship, experiences and background was important to accomplish God's plans. What do we know about Paul from these verses?

Acts 22:3-5

Acts 22:26

Philippians 3:4-6

Look back at all we have learned about Paul. We've seen the good, the bad, and the ugly. But God is using Paul to accomplish His goals in the world. You too may have good, bad and ugly aspects to your life. Do you trust God can use it ALL for His work?

What negatives from your life (sin, suffering, pain) have you seen God use for His glory?

We haven't even scratched the surface of Paul's life. Tomorrow we will continue to look at Paul's life and experiences and how God was able to use him.

Response and/ or prayer:

You have not handed me over to the enemy but have set my feet in a spacious place.

☙ Day 2 ☙

Paul's Ministry

Paul's ministry and the information we have in the Bible about his life are extensive. Covering it all would take many Bible studies! In the middle of his ministry, on his third missionary journey, Paul makes a farewell speech to the Elders at Ephesus. In this speech, he summarizes where he finds himself in ministry. In studying this passage, we can get the feel for a moment in time of Paul's life.

Read Acts 20:17-21. List the actions Paul claims in these verses. What does he say he has done or experienced?

Read 20:22-24. What does Paul say may happen when he goes to Jerusalem?

Why doesn't this scare Paul away and cause him to change his plans?

You have not handed me over to the enemy but have set my feet in a spacious place.

What is the task the Lord has for him according to verse 24?

Read 20:25-31. What warnings or directions does Paul give these church leaders?

Read the rest of chapter, Acts 20:32-38. Why do the leaders grieve at the end of his time with them?

Read through the following lists, noting what events in Paul's life happened before this farewell speech and what events happened after.

Before Acts 20
- Stephen is stoned.
- Paul is called by the Holy Spirit.
- A plot to kill Paul is hatched.
- Barnabas and Paul are worshipped like gods.
- Barnabas and Paul have a sharp disagreement and part ways.
- Paul and Silas are imprisoned.
- Paul is abused by Jews in Jerusalem.

After Acts 20

- Paul goes back to Jerusalem despite great danger.
- Paul is arrested.
- Paul is able to give his testimony to large crowds of people.
- A crowd of 40 men commit to kill Paul.
- Paul is put on trial.
- Paul is shipwrecked on the island of Malta.
- Paul is bit by a snake.
- Paul is confined to house arrest in Rome.

Paul is speaking here in a moment in time. It is *after* some serious difficulties had plagued Paul. It is *before* other serious difficulties plagued Paul. Because we live in a fallen, evil world, we can be assured we are going to face hardships in our future. We also have and will experience triumphs and joy. If we let them, these circumstances can rock our very foundation.

Write Acts 20:24 below.

If you considered your life worth nothing, what struggles, worries, or triumphs would matter less to you?

What do you consider to be the task the Lord Jesus has given you? If you are not sure, pray and ask God for wisdom in this area.

You have not handed me over to the enemy but have set my feet in a spacious place.

At the end of the week, we will look again at what God is calling each of us to do for Him.

Response and/or prayer:

≈ Day 3 ≈

Paul's Identity

Now that we have a picture of some of the major points in Paul's life, let's think about how Paul could have felt about his life, about himself.

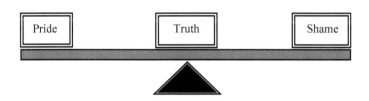

Imagine a teeter-totter. We don't see these much on playgrounds anymore and probably it's a good thing! I remember the hard landing you can take when your partner jumps off their end and you go crashing to the ground. Sometimes one of us would stand in the middle while two other children sat on the ends. While the ends go up and down, the middle stayed pretty much the same and the person could stay there without much movement.

Our feelings about ourselves can be like a teeter-totter. On one day we can be full of pride in ourselves and our accomplishments. *My children are well liked by their teachers! I am well-known at church! I have a clean home! I got a great review at work! I fed my family a home-cooked meal yesterday! I grow a garden! I have great taste! I'm way better than those around me! I don't sin...much!*

If we are high up on the pride side, it doesn't take much to cause us to fall hard and switch to the shame side of the teeter-totter. *My kids are making horrible choices. Someone asked me if I was a visitor at church. My home is a mess. I am overwhelmed at work and am sure I can't do this job. My kids eat fast food. I watch too much TV. I look like a crazy person today. When I remember what I was like at 15 (or 20, or 30, or 40) I'm ashamed. I can't believe I said that. I can't believe I reacted like that. Why can't I stop yelling at my kids?*

On <u>either</u> side of the teeter-totter, we are hearing and believing lies:

- Your worth is in how big your family is.

- Your worth is found in how your kids turn out.

- Your worth is found in your title at work.

- Your worth is found in your parenting/homemaking skills.

- Your worth is found in how much money/possessions you have.

- Your worth is earned by being obedient.

- Your worth is in how people think about you and if they like you.

Without a doubt, either side of the teeter-totter is shaky and unpredictable. In the middle of these two is the truth. Think back to yesterday and reading about Paul's life.

What are some of the events and accomplishments that could have led Paul to feel pride in himself?

What are some of the events and actions that could have led Paul to feel shame in himself?

What do the following verses say about pride?

Proverbs 8:13

Proverbs 11:2

Proverbs 16:18

Proverbs 29:23

Isaiah 25:11

Daniel 4:37

What do the following verses say about shame?

Psalm 25:2

You have not handed me over to the enemy but have set my feet in a spacious place.

John 8:10-11

Romans 10:9-11

1 John 3:19-20

Romans 8:1-2

Was (or is) there a time in your life when you felt prideful or placed your worth in yourself? Describe how that felt and how it ended.

Was (or is) there a time in your life when you felt shamed and placed your worth in yourself? What were some of the lies you told yourself?

What is the truth? We will look in the next couple of days at the truth of your worth by looking at how Paul viewed himself. We will look at the lies you have believed and counter them with truth.

Write down at least one true statement about yourself based on the verses we read about pride and shame.

Response and/or prayer:

Paul's Testimony

P aul's letters make up a good portion of the New Testament. His encouragements and reprimands for his recipients are powerful. God breathed this revelation through Paul and the result is a collection of letters we continue to turn to today. In each letter Paul identified himself at the beginning. These introductions give us a glimpse into his thinking about who he was in Christ. Look at each introduction and write down Paul's self-description.

1 Corinthians 1:1

2 Corinthians 1:1

Galatians 1:1

Ephesians 1:1

Philippians 1:1

Colossians 1:1

1 Timothy 1:1

2 Timothy 1:1

Titus 1:1

Philemon 1:1

What are the common denominators? What can we know about Paul's self-view from these verses?

In these next passages, Paul explains our identity as well as his own. In each passage, write down what we are as followers of Christ.

Romans 8:17

Ephesians 5:8

Philippians 3:20

Colossians 1:13-14

Colossians 2:13

While these passages help us identify ourselves with God's truth, the reality is Paul did not write his letters in order for us to feel good about ourselves. The focus of his letters is always Christ and His amazing mercy and saving grace. So while it is important to think about who we are, it is useless if it doesn't point us to God. We are nothing apart from Him.

You have not handed me over to the enemy but have set my feet in a spacious place.

Write your own introduction like the ones Paul did to begin his letters. What would you say about who you truly are?

Response and/or prayer:

ῶ Day 5 ῶ

Living in Lies or Living in Truth

I was just six years old when I decided I wanted to be a friend of Jesus' forever. Growing up in a family that attended a good church and worshipped God had given me a solid understanding that I needed Jesus to forgive my sins and that I could live with Him forever in heaven. I'm confident Jesus was drawing me to Him from early on in my life. I continued to grow in maturity and in my spiritual walk throughout elementary school. When I was twelve years old, I went to a middle school summer camp and learned this relationship wasn't just here to make me feel good. I made another commitment, a re-commitment to follow God's lead as Lord of my life. I continue to grow in my spiritual walk through both heartaches and blessings.

This is the basic "testimony" I have always told about my relationship with God. Just for fun, go back an circle all the "I"s I used in the previous paragraph. I count eleven! I only mentioned God or Jesus five times. Hmmm…

Let's look at another passage written by Paul. In this passage, Paul is basically giving his testimony. He is reminding the believers in Galatia that he is more qualified to give them truth than the other leaders who were questioning the validity of Paul's message.

Read Galatians 1:11-24.

Just like in my testimony, Paul uses lots of "I"s in the first few verses you read. He is describing his previous way of life. Fill in the missing words from verses 13 and 14.

For you have heard of my previous way of life in Judaism, how

intensely _____ _____ the church of God and tried to

_____ it. ____ was _____ in Judaism beyond many

Jews of my own age and was _____ _____ for the

traditions of my fathers.

You have not handed me over to the enemy but have set my feet in a spacious place.

The focus in these verses is on what Paul accomplished, how he acted and how he compared with others. The next two verses switch the focus.

Who set Paul apart from birth?

Who called Paul by His grace?

Who was pleased to reveal His son in Paul?

Who enabled Paul to preach among the Gentiles?

Paul's testimony, his description of the most important event in his life, and his summary of his transformation is all about God. God is the subject that causes every action in these sentences. Perhaps I need to rethink the way I tell my story. How can I reform it to better reflect that God is the author?

Perhaps my testimony should sound more like this:

God, in His infinite love and boundless grace, drew me close to Himself when I was just six years old. Using many Godly people, Jesus exposed my pride and sin, washed me clean, forgave me and allowed me to have an intimate and close relationship with the creator of the universe. At a critical time in my maturing, God showed me that I was welcome to approach the throne, He considered me family and He made me alive in Him. God uses everything that happens in my life, both the good and the bad, to draw me closer to Him and to work out His good will.

The first testimony isn't wrong. It is perfectly fine. However, taking a moment to acknowledge God as the source of all that happens in our lives is a valuable exercise. The second version is more accurate and I think more meaningful. **Below, write your own story. Imagine you are having coffee with a new friend who asks how you came to hold your beliefs. It doesn't need to be long, just be sure to use God as the subject for each of your sentences.**

In the spacious place, where God gives us rest and protection, we can see the truth about who we are because of the work of Christ on the cross. Knowing the truth about God keeps our view of ourselves in check. It keeps us from getting out of balance and being either full of pride or full of shame. Ultimately, we exist for God's pleasure not our own. The more we take our focus off ourselves and place it on Him, the more clearly we can see the truth.

When your mind, feelings or situation fail to coincide with the freedom, peace, acceptance, protection, truth and transformation of the spacious place, consider the lies or truths you are accepting in your heart.

What lies could keep you from experiencing the spacious place?

In the spacious place, we are enjoying those promises because we have an accurate view of God and an accurate view of ourselves.

Response and/ or prayer:

Week 7: Transformation Not Stagnation

I remember at about 28 or 29 years old thinking it was time to get my act together and figure some things out. I was a slave to my emotions at that time and had the hardest time getting over events that would happen to me. I recognized this as sin and as immaturity. In my mind I knew 30 was around the corner, and I set myself a deadline to conquer these struggles before that birthday. Well, 30 came and went. I was still struggling with trusting God, letting go of powerful emotions, and I badly needed to figure out how to gain some eternal perspective. Sometime in my early thirties I became discouraged seeing the same struggles resurface again and again in my life. Why didn't I have it all together? Why couldn't I be "finished?" I should be a mature Christian. I should have it all figured out. I had been a Christian for over 20 years!

In contrast, I once was in a Bible study group with a beautiful woman named Betty. She was in her late 80s at the time and had lived an unbelievable life. She had known and worked with some of the most famous Christian leaders in the world. She went to college with Billy Graham (she called him Bill). In our discussion one day, Betty said she just wanted to keep growing and changing. This was such an important moment for me. We are never done, never finished growing. What a relief it is to know I can continue to grow closer to God, to grow more Christ-like no matter what age I am. I want to keep growing and changing until the end too. There is danger in believing we have learned it all, or figured it all out. If we think that way, we will stop transforming. Being able to live in the spacious place state of relationship means we must be open to continually grow, continually transform, continually learn and continually change. This week we will study the life and teachings of Peter to see an example of someone who continued to change and grow for his whole life.

MEMORY VERSE:

For if you possess these qualities in increasing measure, they will keep you from

being ineffective and unproductive in your knowledge of our Lord Jesus Christ.

⮞ 2 Peter 1:8

☙ Day 1 ☙

Peter

From the time he was called by Jesus to the end of his days, the apostle Peter was intensely committed to Jesus. Even in his moments of doubt and failure, we see a man who desperately wants to follow Jesus with his whole being. During Christ's ministry on earth, Peter has many opportunities to put his faith into action, and to live out what he believed.

Read Luke 5:1-11. Let's consider what Peter (Simon) may have been thinking on this day.

What had Peter been doing before Christ got in his boat to teach? How do you think he was feeling at this point?

What command does Jesus give Peter (vs. 4)?

Jesus doesn't say they are going to try to catch fish, or see if they can catch fish, or try to find some fish. What does He say instead?

You have not handed me over to the enemy but have set my feet in a spacious place.

Record Peter's response here. What attitude might Peter have had to this command and what might he have been thinking?

The catch of fish is so big and unusual no one could deny it was a miracle! What happens next is the true climax of the story. The reaction of Peter is astounding. **What is it Peter must have realized or been struck by in observing this miracle?**

I am not super careful with laundry. I see care instructions as suggestions. I don't separate colors or types of laundry, it all goes in together. So all our white t-shirts and socks eventually become slightly grey. It isn't so noticeable (at least that is what I tell myself), until I see and old t-shirt next to a brand new one. When I put the slightly grey shirt next to a blue or black shirt, it looks fine; it looks pretty white. But if I put it next to a new white shirt, the level of discoloration becomes evident.

I think this is like what happened to Peter in the boat. Compared to friends, neighbors or co-workers, Peter probably thought he was a pretty good person. It was only when Peter saw his heart next to the perfect white of Christ's heart that he saw the truth. He saw how sinful he was, compared to Jesus.

What dangers are there in comparing yourself to other people?

When have you been caught up in comparing yourself to others? What was the outcome?

What value is there in comparing yourself to Christ?

Does that make you feel uncomfortable? Why or why not?

Now look back at our passage. What does Jesus say to Peter in response?

Jesus calls Peter to continue to follow Him despite his sinfulness, despite his inadequacy. This is the beauty of the gospel. We are all unworthy, yet we all are called to follow Him anyway.

In what ways are you unworthy and yet accepted anyway? Praise God!

Peter shows us in this passage his heart sees the truth. He is a sinner in desperate need of a savior. And despite his realization that he isn't worthy, Peter does follow. He continues to follow Jesus as His disciple, proving again and again he is totally committed; he is all in.

Respond to today's lesson by praising God for the perfection of Jesus. Maybe in the focus on the pure perfection of Christ, some truth about your own heart can start to become visible.

Response and/or prayer:

Big Highs and Big Lows

In Matthew 16, Peter again has an opportunity to prove himself. He confirms and declares who he believes Jesus is. Read Matthew 16:13-20.

What is Peter's answer when Jesus asks who the disciples believe he is?

Jesus had been addressing all the disciples here, but He responds specifically to Peter in verses 17-19. What are some of the elements of His response?

Who is warned not to tell anyone Jesus is the Messiah?

So Peter and the disciples are gaining understanding slowly about who Jesus is and what He came to do. The very next passage in Matthew records another interaction with Peter, in which he doesn't give the right answer. Read Matthew 16:21-28.

You have not handed me over to the enemy but have set my feet in a spacious place.

What is the news Peter is objecting to? What does he think should never happen?

What does Jesus call Peter in verse 23?

Remember He has just commended Peter, and told him he will be absolutely critical in building His church. **Why does Jesus react this way? List as many possibilities as you can.**

The next bit of instruction given by Jesus may help us understand His reaction better. For each verse, what does Jesus ask His followers to do?

Verse 24:

Verse 25:

Verse 26:

Based on this instruction, what does Peter's reaction in verse 22

reveal about his heart condition? What sin is behind his words?

So Peter goes from being blessed by Jesus, commended for his faith and held up as a leader in the movement one day, to being called Satan and called out for his sinful motives another. **How would you have handled this rebuke by Jesus?**

Would you have been tempted to give up, to feel so ashamed by your mistake that you would feel unredeemable? We will continue to look at Peter's life and writings to see how he responded tomorrow.

Talk to God about how willing you are to deny yourself, to lose your life or to forfeit the world.

Response and/or prayer:

You have not handed me over to the enemy but have set my feet in a spacious place.

☙ Day 3 ☞

Willing Spirit, Weak Body

Peter's most famous mistakes are probably his denials. I like Mark's gospel because he is so straightforward in his telling of events. He is to the point! Let's look at Mark's description of the last supper and the events that followed.

Read Mark 14:17-31.

What do you imagine the mood was like during that dinner? Typically Passover week was a celebration. Was this dinner different?

Jesus predicts the betrayal of Judas. Each disciple asks if he is the betrayer. Jesus just says is it is one of them. What a wild moment that must have been. They all accept what Jesus is saying as truth. They trust in His ability to tell what was still to happen in the future. What else does Jesus predict in the following verses:

Verse 25:

Verse 27:

Verse 30:

This time Peter doesn't believe what Jesus is saying. What does he claim in verse 31?

Read Mark 14:32-42. While Jesus is agonizing in the garden, Peter, James and John fall asleep three times. The second time, Jesus addresses Peter specifically. What is the last sentence Jesus says to him in verse 38?

What a great description of Peter and his life! **In what ways is Peter's "spirit willing?" Think of examples from what we have studied.**

In what ways is Peter's "body weak?" How has he shown that when the pressure is on, he fails?

Peter is next mentioned when he cuts off the ear of a soldier during Peter's arrest. Mark's account doesn't identify the man as Peter, but we know it is him from John's account (see John 18:10).

Read Mark 14:43-50. What do you think about Peter's action? What does it tell you about him?

What happens in verse 50? Is Peter included in this?

Read Mark 14:66-72, the passage that describes Peter's three denials. As you read, list what emotions or thoughts might have been going through Peter's mind.

Peter wept after the rooster crowed. Matthew's account says he wept bitterly. Which of the following do you think might have been an possible reaction after this failure?

- O He might have run away and left Jesus and his friends behind.
- O He might have returned to his fishing career.
- O He might have become vocal against those who followed Christ.
- O He might have focused on the accuracy of Jesus' prediction.
- O He might have had a renewed commitment.
- O He might have felt humiliated and not wanted to face the

disciples.
o   Other:

Which of these options do you think you would have been inclined to do? Why?

Tomorrow we will see Peter in the next phase of his life and learn how he handled this failure.

Response and/or prayer:

You have not handed me over to the enemy but have set my feet in a spacious place.

Mystery Encounter

We left off yesterday with the denials of Peter. He had been confident in his commitment to follow Jesus. When the pressure was on, though, Peter turned his back on Jesus. Meanwhile, Jesus was being tried, beaten, and killed on a cross between two criminals.

The book of Luke includes more detail than Mark about the time after Jesus rose from the dead.

Read Luke 24:1-12. Several incredible and unbelievable events happen in a short amount of time to these women. Complete these sentences:

- Instead of a sealed tomb, they saw:

- They were frightened by the appearance of:

- They are shocked and delighted to hear the news that:

Where did they go first with this news? Who was there to hear it?

What was the general consensus among the people who heard?

Peter is singled out from this crowd and had a different reaction. What was it?

Why do you think Peter was "wondering" about what had happened. Does it surprise you at all he didn't realize Jesus was alive? Why?

The next time we hear about Peter is after Jesus appeared to two men on the road to Emmaus. Jesus spends some time with these men, explaining Scriptures, especially those regarding Himself. While they dined with Him, their eyes were opened and they realized who He was. Then Jesus disappears from them. What a story they had to tell!

Read Luke 24:33-35. What can you conclude knowing they took their story first to the Eleven?

Did you catch verse 34? Who is mentioned by name?

You have not handed me over to the enemy but have set my feet in a spacious place.

This little gem of a verse is not explained or described further. Paul confirms it in 1 Corinthians 15:5. Read that verse. I would love to know what that encounter was like! **Why do you think Jesus singled Peter out to appear to him personally?**

What comfort that must have been to Peter. **How might Peter have felt before, during and after Jesus appeared to him personally?**

This gives me such comfort. This encounter, even without details, shows me the gentleness of Jesus. He cared deeply for Peter, and knew how ashamed he was feeling. Jesus gave Peter time. He cared and loved enough to seek him out separately from the rest. Praise God He cares for my tender and bruised heart too.

Response and/or prayer:

Day 5

In Increasing Measure

In the last week, we have studied Peter's life including some of his triumphs and failures. Peter's life was not one of stagnation. He lived a life of transformation. He was continually learning, growing and allowing trials and failures to refine him and bring glory to God. Paul at one point has to reprimand Peter because even in his leadership of the early church, Peter made mistakes.

You will fail. I will fail. If I sin, am I refusing the promise of the spacious place? When I make mistakes, should I become discouraged and wallow in shame? Or should I defend my mistake and refuse to learn from it? NO. The spacious place is a place of transformation, a place where you can continue to make mistakes, grow, learn and change through God's work in your life.

Peter went through his share of difficulties. Some of them were caused by others (for example his imprisonments) and others were caused by his own sin (denying Christ).These did not stop Peter. Peter kept going, kept learning, kept confessing sin. He allowed these difficulties to change him. Here Peter was, one of the chosen inner circle and he was making terrible choices. While Jesus didn't ignore these sins, He also didn't give up on Peter.

Let's look at some of Peter's own words in light of what we know of his life and journey with Christ.

What is the result of suffering, sin or trials according to the following verses:

1 Peter 1:6-7

1 Peter 2:1-2

1 Peter 5:10-11

You have not handed me over to the enemy but have set my feet in a spacious place.

Throughout 1 Peter, suffering is addressed repeatedly. Think about the various ways Peter had suffered in his lifetime. Peter doesn't say these things lightly. What does Peter tell us to do with our suffering in each of these verses?

1 Peter 4:12-13

1 Peter 5:6-7

Let's look at Peter's second letter. Fill in the following from 2 Peter 1:5-7.

For this very reason, make every effort to add to your faith,

And to your goodness,

And to knowledge,

And to self-control,

And to perseverance,

And to godliness,

And to brotherly kindness,

Next to each of the words you wrote, write two or three synonyms or a definition. Use a dictionary or thesaurus if needed.

Which of those qualities do you think are strengths for you, they come easier for you than for others?

Which of those qualities do you think are hard for you, or are areas where you struggle?

Now look at 2 Peter 1:8. I believe a key phrase in this verse can help us understand what transformation should look like in our lives. Peter could have said "For if you possess these qualities, they will keep you from being ineffective and unproductive in your knowledge of the Lord Jesus Christ." What phrase did I leave out from verse 8?

What do you think we can learn from this phrase?

You have not handed me over to the enemy but have set my feet in a spacious place.

Peter does not see our lives as complete or finished when we become Christians. He does not see us as complete or finished when we become mature Christians. The goal here isn't to be perfect all the time, never making mistakes. It is a different outlook. He desires for us to work on these areas *in increasing measure.* It is a growth process.

How does this concept or idea match or not match how you view your growth as a Christian?

How do you normally handle failure?

What changes to your thinking might God be prompting in you right now?

Response and/or prayer:

WEEK 8: TAKING THE SPACIOUS PLACE WITH YOU

We have finally arrived at the final week of study. Thank you for sticking with me through these weeks. I have struggled these last few weeks with the state of the world around me. Saint Louis, my city, experienced an unusual time lately in the wake of a white police officer shooting an unarmed black man. A palpable tension hovered over the city for several weeks prior to the grand jury announcement that they were not going to indict the officer. It was a strange time for me as I heard many rumors and predictions about what might happen or could happen. Lists of targets were released, some of them close to us. In addition to my feelings about the events, I began to feel some real fear. It is humbling to know the fear I felt for a short time is a daily part of the lives of other people all over the world. But this was new to me. I definitely felt unsettled and worried. My anxiety was compounded because I was also writing about how God offers peace. It was a good hard light shining on my faith. Did I really believe God was sovereign? What if something did happen to me or my family? Would I still see God's hand in it? What exactly was causing my fear? Was there an outcome that would make me doubt God's love for me?

The actual outcome, while difficult, violent and angry, was much calmer than many of the predictions and did not touch me or my family directly. Many threats and rumors that had been made did not happen. Now is a good time for me to take a hard look at my reaction to this difficult time. What does it tell me? How much does my head knowledge actually affect the way I think and act?

This week I'm going to challenge you to join me in this self-assessment. Let's gather some of the head knowledge we have gained in this study and see if we can take it a level further, to the heart.

MEMORY VERSE:

> *Therefore, since we are surrounded by such a great cloud of witnesses, let us throw off everything that hinders and the sin that so easily entangles, and let us run with perseverance the race marked out for us. Let us fix our eyes on Jesus, the author and perfecter of our faith, who for the joy set before him endured the cross,*

scorning its shame, and sat down at the right hand of the throne of God. Consider

him who endured such opposition from sinful men so that you will not grow weary

and lose heart.

≈ *Hebrews 12:1-3*

You have not handed me over to the enemy but have set my feet in a spacious place.

Some Encouragement for the Journey

Embarking on a journey can be hard. It can be a bit frightening. You may experience the unknown. We all could use some encouragement for our journey with Christ, our journey towards becoming more like Him.

Read Hebrews 12:1-3.

During this study, we discussed many characters from the Bible. We studied Sarah and Hagar, David, a crippled woman, Joseph, Paul and Peter. **Which of these characters resonated most with you? In what way did you feel a connection?**

Which of these characters is an example you would most like to follow? Why?

Which of the characters made you consider how <u>not</u> to think or act? How?

We are surrounded by a great cloud of witnesses (Hebrews 12:1) who have paved the way, left us with great examples, left us with cautionary tales, who have both pleased and disappointed God. What should our response be to these witnesses according to verse 1?

What are the things that hinder you in your race? What sins easily entangle you?

List all the accomplishments of Jesus according to verses 2-3.

In what way is the work of Jesus on the cross encouraging to you?

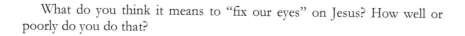

You have not handed me over to the enemy but have set my feet in a spacious place.

What do you think it means to "fix our eyes" on Jesus? How well or poorly do you do that?

Have you experienced a time when you were weary or lost heart? Or are you experiencing that now? What happened?

In your own words, write a sentence or two of encouragement to yourself. What would you say to a friend facing your same situation?

Please be encouraged! The work of Jesus on the cross changes EVERYTHING. He came to put right the world, to bring us righteousness we could never attain on our own. And in coming, being crucified and rising again from the grave, He conquered death. He conquered sin. He made it possible for us to stand before the God of the universe, the creator of the world, the perfect and holy God. Without Him we would have no hope. We would truly be enslaved, full of anxiety, judged for our sins, abandoned, lied to and completely stuck in that place.

That does not have to be our reality! God has offered to place us in a spacious place and we have access to His many promises. This is such good news!

Response and/ or prayer:

You have not handed me over to the enemy but have set my feet in a spacious place.

Contrasts in Beliefs

Today I'm going to ask you to do a lot of thinking. Each column of the following chart will get more difficult. So I suggest you start by filling all of the first column before tackling the other columns. We won't be completing the whole chart in one day. In each block, write a statement that reflects what a person living life in each way would believe is true. The "spacious place gift" means the first attribute in each pair we have studied so far. The "negative alternative" is the second attribute in each pair. So for the first box, write a statement that a person living in freedom would say is true.

Here are some of the possibilities for the first box. These are all statements someone truly living in freedom believes:

- The only thing that matters in life is God's grace and redemption.

- I no longer "have to" participate in sin that used to enslave me.

- God gives me the strength to resist sin.

- God is the only one who guides my life.

- Other influences around me won't sway me from my focus on Jesus.

Don't worry about finding a "right" answer. There are many answers for each box. The goal of this exercise is to get us thinking about what we truly believe. Sometimes what we say does not reflect what we do. Our hearts may be believing, as truth, something we know in our minds is a lie.

After you finish the first column, go back and tackle the second. In this column, you will write what a person who is stuck in that negative way of living would believe is true. What might their actions reveal about their true beliefs? So for the box for slavery, here are some possible answers:

163

- I can't change.

- I have to _____.

- It is important to impress those around me.

- I am a success if the world likes what I do.

- Jesus' redemption is great, but my sin is too deep for His love to cover.

Save the last column for tomorrow. Try to set aside some quiet time tomorrow in which you can really reflect on your life.

You have not handed me over to the enemy but have set my feet in a spacious place.

Contrasting Pairs	Spacious Place Gift	Negative Alternative	Me (what I believe)
Freedom vs. Slavery (Sarah and Hagar)			
Peace vs. Anxiety (David)			
Acceptance vs. Judgment (crippled woman)			

Protection vs. Abandonment (Joseph)			
Truth vs. Lies (Paul)			
Transformation vs. Stagnation (Peter)			

You have not handed me over to the enemy but have set my feet in a spacious place.

Response and/or prayer:

Day 3

What I Believe

We are rapidly coming to the end of the Bible study. Thank you so much for studying with me these last few weeks! Please go back and finish the chart from yesterday. In the final column, I want you to write a sentence that reflects where you are right now. I would imagine most of you want to agree with the statements in your first column. I know it is true I am set free from sin, for example. Yet, my final column might say something like, "I know I am set free from sin but I still think others' opinions of me are important."

We started the study talking about the spacious place as a gift God offers us. We can choose to live with that state of mind, living with freedom, peace, acceptance, protection, truth and transformation. Or we can believe all those are true and available from God but reject them. We can live as slaves, full of anxiety, feeling judged, abandoned, believing lies and remaining stagnant in that place.

Do you remember the place you pictured at the beginning, the place that represented relief and peace to you? The spacious place was a metaphor David used to help us think about and visualize what God is doing for us. Thinking through this metaphor really helped me understand God's gift and love for me. When I am fearful, or a slave to my feelings, or believing the lies of Satan, it helps me to think about the spacious place. I can picture what I am rejecting. Because choosing not to live in the spacious place is a choice. I know the truth; I must live the truth.

Response and/or prayer:

Lessons Learned

I am hoping you will take some more time for self-assessment today. Yesterday you completed the table focusing on what you personally believe is true. Below, write a prayer for each category we have studied. Some may be praise, some may be confession, some may be commitment. Consider what you wrote in the table about your own beliefs. Think about where you were when you started the study, where you are now, and where you'd like to be. This is a chance to sit in the presence of God and hear from Him about your life, actions, thoughts and beliefs.

Freedom not slavery (Sarah and Hagar)

Peace not anxiety (David)

Acceptance not judgment (the crippled woman)

Protection not abandonment (Joseph)

Truth not lies (Paul)

Transformation not stagnation (Peter)

I will be glad and rejoice in your love, for you saw my

affliction and knew the anguish of my soul. You have not

handed me over to the enemy but have set my feet in a

spacious place.

Thank you Lord, for saving us from our enemies and setting our feet in a spacious place. Give us the courage to look deeply inward and see if we are accepting or rejecting this offer. You are so good and faithful. Continue to transform us into your likeness, in increasing measure day by day. Amen.

Response and/or prayer:

The Cry of Your Heart

L ook back at the first week of study, week 1, day 1. We looked at this passage from Ephesians; a prayer of Paul for the people of that church. Read Ephesians 1: 17-23 again:

"I keep asking that the God of our Lord Jesus Christ, the glorious Father, may give you the Spirit of wisdom and revelation, so that you may know him better. I pray also that the eyes of your heart may be enlightened in order that you may know the hope to which he has called you, the riches of his glorious inheritance in the saints, and his incomparably great power for us who believe. That power is like the working of his mighty strength, which he exerted in Christ when he raised him from the dead and seated him at his right hand in the heavenly realms, far above all rule and authority, power and dominion, and every title that can be given, not only in the present age but also in the one to come. And God placed all things under his feet and appointed him to be head over everything for the church, which is his body, the fullness of him who fills everything in every way."

These were the desires I have been praying for all who decide to join me in this Bible study.

1. I desire for you to have the Spirit of wisdom and revelation.

2. I desire for you to know Him better.

3. I desire for this Bible study to enlighten you in some way through the work of the Holy Spirit.

4. I desire for you to know hope.

5. I desire for you to know you are called by God.

6. I desire for you to know the riches of your inheritance.

7. I desire for you to see His great power.

8. I desire for you to trust in that great power.

Which of these did you circle back in week 1, indicating a deep desire of your heart for yourself?

Has the Lord, through the Holy Spirit, touched that desire during the course of this study? How?

Has the Lord given you any of the other of these desires? Has He shown Himself to be faithful in any of these areas? How?

If you didn't experience growth through this study, why do you think that is? Is there a change you could make that could open your heart wider to the promptings of the Lord?

Glance back through the study now. Can you think of three main ideas or points that really made an impression with you?

1.

2.

3.

I'm so proud of you for sticking with me all the way to the end. May the Lord continue to bless you and grow you day by day into an increasing likeness of Him. May you find the beauty of dwelling with God in the spacious place!

You have not handed me over to the enemy but have set my feet in a spacious place.

WHAT'S STOPPING US?

How are you doing living a life of freedom, peace, acceptance, truth, protection and transformation? What kind of obstacles are keeping you from living out this idea of the spacious place? Here are a few of the major obstacles I have faced and a few suggestion for you if you find yourself in this place.

Discouragement:

Feeling discouraged about your spiritual life or growth is one of the obstacles I sometimes face when trying to grow closer to God. I can be discouraged about my lack of growth because it can be difficult to see the small steps you are taking in coming closer to God. Sometimes my circumstances are discouraging. I feel sad and worn out by the struggle in my life.

What can you do?

1. Seek out encouragement. Others in your life can help you gain perspective on your circumstances and moods. Be open and honest with friends and family about how discouraged you feel, and then allow them to encourage you. Surround yourself with others who are hopeful and positive about life and spiritual things. This is an important role of the church. We are to encourage each other.

2. Focus on the positive. Take time to remember the ways God has worked in and through you over your life. Write them down, tell others about them, or write a letter about them to someone else who also may need encouragement. Make a scrapbook or a piece of art. Get creative! The goal is to remind yourself of the faithfulness of the Father.

3. Resist the urge to check out. When I'm discouraged I tend to want to ignore the feeling and watch TV. It does get me through the next hour, but it isn't feeding my soul. Turn instead to music, scripture, or serving others. Work on a hobby or something else that feeds you. Pray. Have a good cry if you need it.

I've used the word discouraged instead of depressed on purpose. I am no expert on the subject of depression, I only can speak from my own experiences. If it is helpful to you, here are my two cents on the subject. I would encourage anyone feeling depressed to check in with a doctor to assess what is happening. Clinical depression or depressive disorder are medical conditions that require medical attention. In my experience there are multiple ways to address depression and all of them should be considered. Okay, I've said my piece!

Distraction:

The list of possible distractions in our lives is long and varied. Some are good, some are bad, some just kill time. We tend to live life at full speed. Every spare minute is filled with entertainment. Even waiting at a stopping light, I find myself wanting to check my phone for emails or messages. There used to be downtime in life. But with smartphones and tablets and laptops, it is all portable now and it seems to go with us everywhere. I love all this technology and I don't think it is all bad. I just need to keep checking in thoughtfully with my usage of it.

What can you do?

1. Use your technology to keep you in scripture regularly. Apps, online Bibles, or devotions can all be accessed in lieu of other entertainment that grabs your attention. Use an alarm on your phone to remind you when you intend to read your Bible. Keep a list of prayer requests on your devices.

2. Take some time to figure out what your distractions are and where you can eliminate some of them. Consider making changes. Make rules for yourself and ask someone to hold you accountable to them.

3. Plan some quiet or silent time into your life. It doesn't need to be a regular discipline to make an impact.

Discontentment:

Discontentment may be the worst of the obstacles in my life. I feel frustrated with myself and then that spills over to everyone else in my life. Or I hear about something someone else has accomplished and I wish I could accomplish more. I spend time looking online for craft and decorating ideas and mine don't turn out like the picture. When I'm discontent I tend to shop for something new. Or I try harder to meet some imaginary goal. But I rarely acknowledge the discontentment and resolve to do something about it.

You have not handed me over to the enemy but have set my feet in a spacious place.

What can you do?

1. Make a list of blessings. This is not a brilliant new idea, but I include it because it works. Pray through them, acknowledging God's blessing in each one.

2. Reframe your complaints. Take each frustration and figure out a way you can be thankful for it. Then do that...thank God for it. For example, instead of being frustrated with a small house, thank God for less house to clean. Instead of being frustrated with a potty training toddler, be thankful your child is healthy enough to learn. Instead of being discontent with a boring job, be thankful for the growth you are experiencing through the challenge. Instead of focusing on your spouse's shortcomings, focus on the characteristics that made you fall in love in the first place. Instead of being discontent with your physical appearance, celebrate the ways God has created you to be unique.

3. Read about the struggles facing women in other parts of the world. Pray for them, and remember their struggles as you go about your day.

FACILITATOR'S GUIDE

S
tudying the Bible in community can add significant value to the study. Hearing how God is working in the lives of others can be a wonderful encouragement. Receiving feedback on your own experiences can clarify where God is at work in your own life. I would love to see this study being used by small groups of people to enhance the experience of going through *The Spacious Place*. Below I've listed some suggestions to help a facilitator know where to start. Please use them in any way that makes sense for your group. Plan to meet nine times – first to introduce the study and then each week thereafter to discuss the week's homework.

For all the sessions:

- Consider finding a way to worship briefly together. Singing, reading scripture, and sharing answers to prayer can all be ways to worship.
- In my opinion, sharing some good food is a great way to become comfortable with each other and fellowship together. It doesn't have to be complicated or fancy. When I did this study for the first time with a group of trusted friends, I served coffee and a little bit of fruit each week.
- Take time to share prayer requests before or after your discussion. Practice being vulnerable before each other and sharing each other's' burdens.
- Open and close each session with prayer, focusing the purpose and dedicating the time to the Lord.

First Session: Introduction

During this session, you will likely be passing out the books, setting up some guidelines for the study and getting to know each other. Here are a few get-to-know-you type questions I have found helpful in breaking the ice without causing discomfort. Remember when we share family statistics, job information or where we live, some may struggle, not having a family, job or an impressive address. In addition, asking about what other Bible studies a person has completed can be intimidating for those just starting to study. Just like we'd never ask everyone to reveal their weight, other questions can be just as uncomfortable for some. We can get caught up in sharing where we serve in the church or community and it all may be misinterpreted as bragging. A little sensitivity can go a long way in making people feel welcome and comfortable.

You have not handed me over to the enemy but have set my feet in a spacious place.

Here are a few conversation starters to try:

- What was your favorite age to be and why?
- What is one thing you always put in your grocery cart?
- How many siblings do you have and what was your birth order?
- What was the last book/movie you read or saw and what did you think?
- What was your favorite thing to do when you were 10 years old?
- What would be your last meal if you knew you were dying tomorrow?
- What is your biggest pet peeve?
- Do you remember a favorite outfit from your childhood? What did it look like?
- What surprised you most when you were in your late teens, early twenties about being a grown up?

In addition to getting to know each other, I suggest reading through the introduction together and glancing through the study to become familiar with the format.

Second Session, discussing Week 1: The Spacious Place

If you can, gather some props that might be associated with the images your group members may have imagined for their spacious places. A straw hat, tiny drink umbrella, ski hat, flower, sunscreen, scarf, fire log, mittens, coffee cup, some sand, pillow, novel could all work. Some pictures to represent mountains, cities, a party, an open meadow, a forest, or a beach would add some more options. Ask the group members to pick one item that could represent his or her spacious place. Go around the group and for each member, try to guess what they imagined. Then ask them to describe it in three words.

Third Session — discussing Week 2: Freedom not Slavery

Bring 3x5 cards and markers. Ask the group to think back to the illustration of a brick wall between you and God representing what can enslave us. Ask the group members to write on each notecard something that can enslave us and keep us from seeing God's hand. These can be ideas from the lesson or from their own life experiences. Tape the cards to a wall or whiteboard in a brick pattern to illustrate the slavery we can experience. Discuss what looking at the wall evokes in each of you. How does it make you feel? What are the keys to tearing down the walls in our own lives?

Fourth Session – discussing Week 3: Peace not Anxiety

Ask the group to think of someone they know who exemplifies peace and someone who exemplifies anxiety. Make two lists on a white board or easel of characteristics of each kind of person. Talk about what the lists bring up in you emotionally. Ask the group to consider where they are and where they want to be on the chart.

Fifth Session – discussing Week 4: Acceptance not Judgment

Bring three large pieces of paper or card stock and markers. Put one on the floor in the middle of the room. Tape one to a wall and another as high as you can on the wall. Pass out the markers and invite the group members to write words on each paper. On the paper on the ground, write down words that express what it is like to have your gaze stuck downward. These will be words of immediate concerns, self-centered problems, or worldly discomforts. On the paper on the wall, ask the group to write messages of accusation they have heard or experienced. When everyone has had a chance, read through the words and sentences on the papers. Then together decide what should be written on the paper high up, representing the upward gaze toward God. Discuss with the group why we fail to constantly keep our gaze upward. What are the struggles and difficulties they experience?

Sixth Session – discussing Week 5: Protection not Abandonment

If you can, share a story with your group about a time when you felt lonely or abandoned. Ask your group to share stories of moving far away from home or stories of feeling lonely. How does it feel? What did you do? How did you change it? Where was God in your situation? How did He show Himself to you? Lead the discussion back to Joseph and his "unplanned" international move.

Seventh Session – discussing Week 6: Truth not Lies

You have not handed me over to the enemy but have set my feet in a spacious place.

Draw the image of the teeter-totter from day 3 on the board or a large piece of paper. Underneath that chart on day 3, there are examples of sources of both pride and shame in italics. Ask the group to name sources of pride or shame they have seen in their lives and relationships. What are ways we see people feeling pride for things that don't matter? What are ways we see people feeling shame for things that don't matter?

Eighth Session – discussing Week 7: Transformation not Stagnation

The profile on Peter in my Life Application Study Bible (p.1595) lists this as one of the lessons from Peter's life. Read this to the group.

"It is better to be a follower who sometimes fails than one who

fails to follow."

Discuss why it sometimes seems better to not follow at all than to follow and stumble. Has anyone ever made that choice? What happened?

Ninth Session – discussing Week 8: Taking the Spacious Place with You

This is the final week of the study, so a celebration of sorts is certainly in order! If you are so inclined, consider creating a gift for your group members with the spacious place scripture. A bookmark, mug, small flower pot, or framed print out would all be lovely things to give that will allow each participant to remember what you studied together. Be sure to allow plenty of time for sharing from the study.

ABOUT THE AUTHOR

Kathy Erickson is a child of God, wife to Dave, mother to three teens. She has always loved church and the Bible. Thanks to the generous and loving mentoring of several wise women at Blackhawk Church in Madison, WI, she was privileged to pursue Bible teaching in women's ministries. Now living in Saint Louis, MO, she loves quiet mornings by the fire petting the world's quirkiest dog, Frog. She has also been a middle school teacher, school librarian and stay at home mom. Writing this study has been a labor of love and a reflection of the personal growth God is working out in her.

Made in the USA
Las Vegas, NV
07 September 2021